SMOKE COOKERY

Georgia Orcutt

A SIGNET BOOK

NEW AMERICAN LIBRARY

TIMES MIRROR

SIGNET TRADEMARK REG. U.S. PAT. OFF. AND FOREIGN COUNTRIES
REGISTERED TRADEMARK—MARCA REGISTRADA
HECHO EN CHICAGO, U.S.A.

SIGNET, SIGNET CLASSICS, MENTOR, PLUME AND MERIDIAN BOOKS
are published by The New American Library, Inc.,
1301 Avenue of the Americas, New York, New York 10019

FIRST SIGNET PRINTING, JUNE, 1978

2 3 4 5 6 7 8 9

PRINTED IN THE UNITED STATES OF AMERICA

Contents

Introduction

As civilization moved from one stage to another, it is indeed unfortunate that cooks with pens were not present to chronicle each advance and record their own thoughts on new trends in the culinary world.

But a cursory review of the history of food does show that smoke cookery, in one form or another, has been known to man for thousands of years.

If you have ever wandered about in a museum and paused to study ancient hieroglyphics and examples of very early art, chances are you've seen at least one simple figure depicted in front of a fire, holding a piece of food over smoking coals. Although authorities can tell us that this early man was shorter than you are, had smaller bones than you do, and lived fewer years than you will, he was essentially practicing the same type of cooking that you can try today.

The Greeks and Romans, as well as the Early Chinese, evidently appreciated what smoking over coals did to food. The culinary connoisseurs of ancient Rome head the list for their far-ranging experiments with roasted and grilled foods.

Lucullus, famed for his incredible orgies, is said to have once served a dish composed of the grilled tongues of 5,000 larks—all of which had first been trained to speak!

Closer to home, smoking and curing were developed in America as ways to both preserve and flavor food. Prior to the introduction of canning in the mid-nineteenth century and, later, the advent of the refrigerator and freezer, smoking was *the* method for keeping pork, beef, and fish.

Curing hams became a specialty of the southern United States when this country was still very young. Smithfield, Virginia, established around 1612, produced smoked hams that became famous as far away as Europe. The enterprising colonists realized a secret in feeding their pigs peanuts, using apple, hickory, and oak for heavy smoking, and aging the cured product for one to two years. Prize Smithfield hams were presented as gifts to presidents and visiting dignitaries, and the tradition has continued.

As self-sufficient pioneer families spread their roots from coast to coast, the smokehouse or meat house came to play an important role on farms of any size, first throughout the eastern United States and then in the Midwest and West.

Although modern technology and life-styles make the smokehouse a thing of the past for most twentieth-century devotees of smoked foods, a burgeoning array of backyard smokers and cookers has been developed for smoke cooking and smoke flavoring of all kinds of foods, from hamburgers to roasts and whole birds.

This book sets out to inform readers about smoked foods and the many ways they can become a part of your culinary experience at home.

Chapter 1.
Basic Smoking Processes

Smoking was originally developed as a preservative method—to dry cuts of meat, flavor them, and keep them edible over the winter and on long journeys.

As a food smokes, whether it is beef, pork, lamb, bacon, poultry, or fish, part of its moisture content slowly evaporates (a preservative method in itself) and its flavor is enhanced by the essence of whatever fuel is used. There are almost as many variables in the equipment, rules of procedure, and fuels for smoking as there are in the foods that can be smoked.

In general, however, there are two basic methods for preparing successful smoked foods.

Hot-Smoking

When foods are exposed to temperatures ranging from 100° to 250°F., they become partially or completely cooked at the same time, and are called "hot-smoked." Basically the same process as barbecuing, hot-smoking can be done on

5

backyard cooking grills, and with several kinds of electrical appliances designed specifically for smoking, including the icebox electric smoker explained in Chapter 3. Hot-smoking requires only a minimal amount of smoke, and most meats and fish can be processed with this method in a matter of hours. (Fish that is hot-smoked is said to be "kippered.") Hot-smoked foods take on a recognizable smoked flavor, but they are sometimes susceptible to spoiling and should be eaten immediately. Once prepared for a meal, any uneaten or extra portions of hot-smoked foods should be refrigerated and kept no longer than ordinary leftovers.

Cold-Smoking

Large commercial food companies "cold-smoke" their products by exposing them to dense smoke for a longer period of time at temperatures under 100°F., sometimes as low as 65°F. Smokehouses and barrel-type smokers that you might operate yourself also utilize this form of smoking, as did colonial settlers in America who often built a smoking oven in their homes or equipped their chimneys with meat hooks.

Hams are perhaps the most popular cold-smoked item in this country; in Europe, the delightful hard sausages so well suited to picnics and traveling have often been cold-smoked. Cold-smoking is also used on foods that would suffer from extreme heat, such as cheeses, some fish, and shellfish.

Smoking Procedure

If a food has been properly smoked by either of the two methods, its color, flavor, and texture will change and it becomes less (but not totally) resistant to spoilage.

Prior to smoking, freshly butchered meats should be cured (see Chapter 4). Curing in itself, apart from smoking, has preservative properties. When the two methods are combined, they give any product a longer life.

After the food has been adequately cured, soak it for at least half an hour to remove excess brine; then scrub it well, using hot water for the best color, and hang it overnight to drip dry. (If you introduce a wet cut to a smokehouse, it will take on a blotchy appearance and will frequently smudge.)

For the best results, string the cuts you wish to smoke; secure hams and shoulders through the shank; bacon and poultry should be reinforced with skewers or wire to keep them in relatively the same position.

Select the fuel of your choice and build a fire in your smoking apparatus. When the temperature reaches 100° to 120°, hot enough to affect the surface grease on the meat, open the ventilators, air holes, or lids. Watch the temperature and the fuel, and adjust draft openings as necessary. A fire that is too hot can ruin the meat, and dense smoke is not essential—a thin cloud of smoke produces the same results as a thick cloud.

A smokehouse, like a good fireplace, works best on cool days—just above freezing to about 55°. Colder or warmer weather may create unpredictable conditions, such as fires that are difficult to regulate, or foods that do not dry at the proper rate as they are smoked.

Precautions While Smoking

Don't leave a smokehouse fire unattended if you are unsure of the temperature it can maintain. If a blaze begins suddenly and the temperature rises quickly, deaden the fire with green sawdust. This will also increase the smoke output.

Store smoked food carefully. Flys can invade even the tightest of smokehouses when the door opens and closes, and they can leave eggs on any kind of food. Wrap, bag, and hang meat separately, and store it in a dry, dark, cool place.

Don't discard smoked meat if surface mold appears. To retard such growth, coat cuts with an edible oil such as linseed or olive oil after the smoking process, and repeat oiling every four or five weeks.

Don't keep bacon as long as other cuts. To be safe, eat it within two months of smoking.

Chapter 2.
Ready-Made Smokers

In the past few years, the backyard cooker market has expanded from the simple grill and hibachi (both, incidentally, can "smoke" foods very nicely) to a fleet of modern units that place a revolutionary new emphasis on smoked foods.

Although a hamburger cooked over one of these new machines is not in the same class as a Smithfield ham, it has, nonetheless, been smoked if prepared a certain way for flavor's sake alone.

At the time of this writing, more than a dozen companies in the United States are manufacturing specialty smoke cookers—charcoal-powered, electric, and gas.

Before investing in a new piece of cooking equipment, consider your needs and decide which kind of grill or smoker is best suited to your life-style. Any grill made will serve you well if the extent of your culinary repertoire is steak, hamburgers, and hot dogs. If roasts and whole birds whet your appetite, select a model that comes equipped with a rotisserie and a hood.

Also think about where you will do most of your cooking. If you dream of secluded cookouts for two in the mountains or at the oceanside, don't foolishly invest in a 200-pound smoker that needs an electric outlet for power!

Choices of what to buy range from compact models as small as eighteen inches high and weighing only a few pounds to large, built-for-a-crowd versions weighing more than 100 pounds that can grill a dozen hamburgers and three chickens all at once.

The different kinds of smokers currently available are outlined below, and many are shown in the photo insert. For further details, consult the list of manufacturers on pages 190–92 and write to the companies for copies of their product literature.

Cast-Iron Grills

One kind of smoker and grill features cast-iron cooking grates with concave undersides to keep grease from splattering. Mounted on wide-tread wheels, these cookers also feature a sealing lid and heat indicator to allow for precise temperature control. An automatic temperature control, a feature accessory with these grills, maintains a pre-set temperature for two to five hours.

Gas Grills

Comparable to a real oven, a gas grill is powered by a liquid propane LP tank and regulators. The smallest portable model uses one pound of fuel; tanks on the larger models hold from eleven to twenty pounds.

The cooking flame on gas cookers is regulated by a control knob, and some models feature lids that can also be raised to different heights for further control of the food as it cooks.

Charcoal-Water Smokers

Available as single- or double-grill smokers, these sophisticated cookers provide a space in the bottom for hardwood fuel; some can hold up to twenty-five pounds of food at a time, including whole birds and large roasts, and can provide up to twelve hours of continuous cooking time. A container of water above the coals and just under the meat reduces shrinkage and keeps food from burning; it also acts as a self-baster.

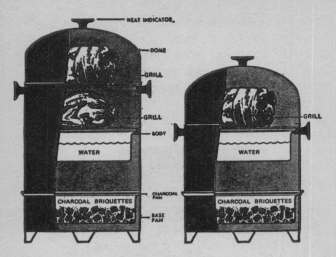

HEAT INDICATOR.

DOME

GRILL

GRILL

BODY

WATER

CHARCOAL BRIQUETTES

CHARCOAL PAN

BASE PAN

GRILL

WATER

CHARCOAL BRIQUETTES

Courtesy of Bosman Industries, Inc.

Metal Grills

Using the same basic cooking method as standard, conventional backyard grills, the newer steel and aluminum models of grills that can be used for smoking come in a variety of colors and feature such adaptations as multipurpose cooking grids with from two to fifteen levels, so that food can be cooked both well done and rare at the same time.

Construction designs encompass a variety of styles, including standard four-leg models with or without wheels, and pedestal bases on wheels. Hood vents and adjustable settings make it possible to regulate air and smoke flow. Some models also feature elevated fuel grates for easy clean-up and more even heat. Some smokers of this kind also come equipped with rotisserie rods for even cooking and quick smoking of large cuts of meat.

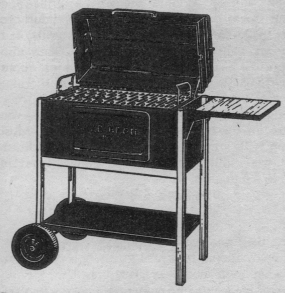

Courtesy of W. C. Bradley Co.

Camp Grills

Featured items in most outdoor and camping supply stores, portable picnic-type grills and camp stoves generally have a shorter endurance rate than more elaborate models of grills, but they are lightweight and inexpensive. They also will do a satisfactory job of processing just about any smokable food product. What you sacrifice in space—most small grills will cook only enough food for two people at one time—you make up for in economy and portability. Most camp grills are manufactured with a plated finish and, when fully assembled, weigh anywhere from five to ten pounds.

Electric Smokers

Several companies manufacture smokers that operate on regular household current and create smoke without an open fire. They are self-regulating and require less attention than other models. Designed for use on patios, balconies, porches, driveways, boats, or campers (within reach of an outlet, but not recommended for use with an extension cord), such smokers, made from aluminum and steel, can handle from fif-

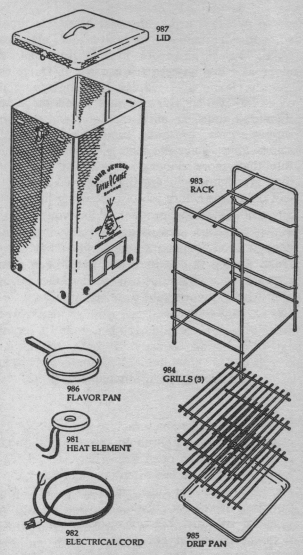

987
LID

983
RACK

984
GRILLS (3)

986
FLAVOR PAN

981
HEAT ELEMENT

982
ELECTRICAL CORD

985
DRIP PAN

Courtesy of Luhr Jensen & Sons, Inc.

teen to twenty-five pounds of meat at one time, and can maintain temperatures as high as 160°F. The newest models include directions for indoor use, but be sure to read the instructions carefully. Some also feature their own special "rocks," to which you can add wood chips to produce genuine smoke.

Accessories

Smoker grills can be used without any of the accessories that are manufactured and sold as companion pieces. But some of the extras can save you time and energy and can increase the use of the grill as well as expand your menus.

The following list will give you an idea of the extent to which the industry has gone in recent years. For details of any of these, or similar items, write to the individual companies given in the manufacturers' listing on pages 190–92.

Basic Tools

Heat from embers can cause severe burns, so it is a good idea to always use several basic tools. A long-handled fork and a long-handled spatula are good and sensible accessories. If you are basting and spooning sauces over meat as it cooks, a spoon or ladle with a long handle and a special brush are also handy tools to have. Several companies manufacture these and others designed specifically for use on grills. A pot holder or mitt is also useful.

Shelves

Custom-made shelves can be ordered for all of the larger models of grills. Made of materials such as redwood, aluminum, hardwood, and for-

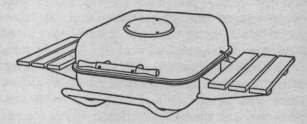

Courtesy of Neosho Products Company

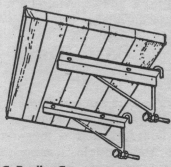

Courtesy of W. C. Bradley Co.

mica, they serve as side tables and provide valuable extra space and cutting board surfaces around the cooking area. Some can be raised and lowered on hinges, and several models are equipped with as many as three shelves—one on either side of the grill and one below.

Rotisseries

A standard addition to just about every grill, rotisserie units are electrical attachments that keep the food you are smoking rotating evenly over the source of heat. Especially useful for hams, large cuts of meat, and whole birds, they come with special clamps to secure the food in position. A rotisserie basket is a specialized version of this accessory that makes it possible to cook small, individual pieces of food such as shrimp, ribs, etc., using rotation methods. Racks for potatoes, corn, and items you may want to warm, such as breads and vegetables, are also available as grill attachments.

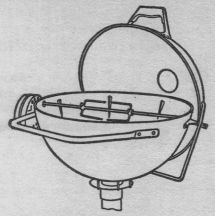

Courtesy of Neosho Products Company

Courtesy of W. C. Bradley Co.

Multi-Wheel Units

Special attachments for individual foods include hot dog wheels and shish kebab wheels. These devices have spokes of appropriate size for even grilling of either food. They also eliminate the need for constant supervision and turning.

Covers

If you plan to leave your grill outdoors where it may be exposed to rain and sun, a cover is a wise investment. Most manufacturers offer custom-tailored vinyl and plastic covers for ten dollars or less. With some models, a heavy-duty trash bag or pieced-together plastic shower curtain will work well also.

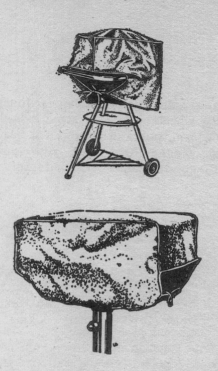

Courtesy of W. C. Bradley Co.

Cleaners

Several products make after-meal clean-up just a little bit easier. These include foam grill cleaners and specially made wire grill brushes for heavy-duty scouring.

Fuels

The kind of fuel you use in your smoker will affect the quality of the finished product and can make a big difference in the taste, texture, and color of whatever food you are cooking.

Natural Fuels

In general, hardwood makes better fuel than softwood. Avoid pine and other woods from conifers: they produce a resinous, strong-smelling sooty smoke that makes a mess and ruins the flavor of meat.

Hickory is the most popular of all smoking fuels, both for the way it burns and for the delightful aroma that it gives to the air and to the food it spends time with. But since hickory has become more expensive and difficult to find in some parts of the country, professional smokehouse operators also burn an assortment of hardwood fuels: beech, buttonwood, apple, peach and other fruitwoods, maple, and pecan (a relative of hickory).

Some people have switched to the abundant red oak, which they feel works as well as any other fuel. Other pros use corn cobs because of their unique flavoring qualities, and because they ignite quickly.

It is also a good idea to keep a barrel full of sawdust, which you can obtain from a local sawmill or make yourself with a shredder, to use for extra smoke or for tempering a blaze. Green sawdust is especially good to deaden a fire that has become hotter than you originally intended. (You can also apply a mist of water and moisten the fuel ever so slightly for additional smoke.)

Green, unseasoned wood will produce more smoke than very dry, aged wood, but if it is too new, it will not burn at all. Most hardwoods can be successfully burned later on in the same year that they are cut.

You can use whole logs, chips, or small branches of wood for your fire. To get the greatest mileage from cut fuels, the USDA suggests arranging the fuel Indian fashion, with individual sticks or logs coming off the center like spokes in a wheel. This pattern causes the fire to become lower and cooler as it burns, an ideal situation for smoking. Be sure to let the fuel burn down to coals before exposing your food to it.

Commercially Prepared Fuels

Prepackaged briquets for use with grills are sold in five-, ten-, and twenty-pound bags, in discount stores, drugstores, supermarkets, garden supply shops, and hardware stores. In addition to the ubiquitous charcoal, a number of other fuels for smoking come prepackaged and are readily

Briquettes must be spread evenly for uniform heat.

DO NOT PILE briquettes against side of kettle.

Courtesy of W. C. Bradley Co.

obtainable. (Some grill manufacturers have developed their own brand of specialty fuels and rocklike products that they recommend for use with their equipment.)

Several businesses make only fuels and offer a variety of items: blended hardwood and hickory chips and flakes, oak briquets, mesquite chips and chunks, and solid pieces of charcoal.

Experiment with different kinds as you cook, using your nose and your wallet as guides. If you are an active practitioner of energy-saving, you might be interested to note that one pound of briquets can produce from 11,000 to 13,000 BTU's of energy.

You can also add flavoring agents to fuels to obtain some interesting results. Juniper berries enhance the aroma of the smoke, and you can also make your own pungent and effective herb smoke by placing several pieces of tarragon, savory, dill, sage, or thyme on the coals.

Chapter 3.

Smokers You Can Build

If your interest in smoked foods becomes more than an occasional urge to taste a tangy ham, consider making your own smokehouse and curing and smoking meats at home on your own. When you process your own foods, you know what has gone into them and what chemicals have been used to cure them. And, in addition to saving money, you will become involved in a new and rewarding hobby.

A perfectly satisfactory, albeit makeshift, smokehouse can be made by converting a barrel, an icebox, or an old refrigerator into a device to smoke a few rashers of bacon, several dozen sausages, or a whole pig. (Large cuts of meat and whole slaughtered animals can be purchased from most meat wholesalers.)

Some make-it-yourself smokehouses are described in the following pages. Before investing time and money in any of these, or others of your own design, check the laws in your city and town concerning burning and smoking.

Barrel Smokers

A portable smoker can readily be adapted from a fifty-gallon metal drum or wooden barrel of comparable size.

Carefully scrub the inside of the container you choose, avoiding those that may have been used to store chemicals or other toxic substances. Wash it down inside and out with a strong detergent, and give it time to dry naturally outdoors in the sun and air.

If the barrel does not have an open end, cut one with a cold chisel or take it to a welding shop and ask someone there to remove an end. After the end is cut away, re-size it to measure approximately three inches less than the diameter of the drum. (This piece becomes a baffle.) If you did not have a top in the beginning, cut a piece of sheet metal to this measurement.

Drill or punch four holes around the circumference of the drum, twelve to fourteen inches from the top. Attach the baffle at this point by means of "L" brackets bolted to the inside. The baffle will regulate the smoke exposure and keep the food from cooking too fast.

Cut a small section, approximately seven by ten inches, at the bottom of the drum to provide access to the fire pit. If you wish, fashion a sheet-metal door with hinges (this step is a flourish that you can bypass without consequence).

Make a grill to hold the food, and suspend it, as you did the baffle, with "L" brackets approximately six inches from the top of the drum.

Make a cover of metal or wood to fit snugly on the drum to keep the smoke from escaping.

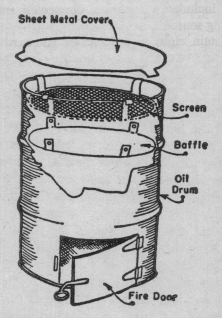

Courtesy of Smokey Smoker Plans

Barrel Smokehouse

A more sophisticated apparatus for smoking utilizes a barrel, as mentioned previously, or a tightly seamed box (both ends removed) which also includes a separate, connected smoke-producing source.

Obtain eight to ten feet of standard stove or tile pipe to make the connecting flue or smokeline. Treat the drum or box as mentioned for the barrel smoker, and remove both ends.

Dig a sloping trench approximately eight to ten feet long and deep enough to cover the pipe, to connect the two structures (see diagram). For the greatest success, design the system so that the fire is at a lower elevation than the barrel. (To finish the system off, cover this pipe with soil, so it cannot be seen.)

Next, dig a fire pit at least two feet deep. Pack the earth around its sides, or line it with stones, bricks, or tempered cement. Mound the earth around the edges of the pit, and cover it with a piece of sheet metal that you can raise and lower as necessary to regulate the heat of the fire.

Run several strips of wood or wire across the top of the drum, or place broomstick handles or large dowels across the top. This will also provide a necessary space to hang the meat you are smoking.

Make a wooden cover that can sit on top of

the barrel, but leave open the space occupied by the dowels or broomsticks. Stretch cheesecloth, muslin, or burlap over the opening to allow smoke to escape and also to protect the meat from insects and dust.

Make lids for both the barrel and the pit, and experiment by raising and lowering each when the fire is going so that you understand how to regulate the smoke and the heat.

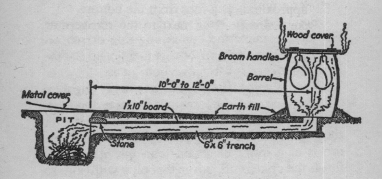

Courtesy of U.S. Department of Agriculture

Refrigerator Smoker

Obtain an old, used refrigerator with a relatively good seal. Remove any galvanized metal parts (compartment doors, bars, trays, etc.). With a suitable drill, cut a five- to eight-inch hole in one wall, approximately a foot from the bottom.

Make a firebox to fit next to the refrigerator. Use a small barrel or make a more permanent structure from cinderblocks or bricks. If possible, secure it to the refrigerator so it can't be knocked over or moved. Leave a hole in the box at a point that corresponds to the hole in the refrigerator. Place a vent at the opening which will connect the two parts, and allow another hole, with vent, on the opposite side of the firebox.

Design a tight-fitting lid for the firebox, and a tray or container to hold the fuel. (The container is not essential, but it will facilitate refueling and clean-up.)

Drill several holes through the refrigerator at corresponding heights, and pass broomstick handles or dowels through them, from which to suspend the food.

Icebox Smoker

Authentic, old-fashioned iceboxes, the forerunners of today's refrigerators, command high prices on the antiques market and are rarely suited for use other than as decorators' items. But if you come across one with an unsalvageable finish, or other irreparable structural problems, or a metal version that isn't as glamorous as the wooden makes, this too can be converted into a homemade smokehouse.

Remove any trays or racks from the storage compartment and adjust them to fit in the upper compartment, where the ice originally was stored. Drill a hole through the top of the icebox, large enough to hold a short length of one-inch water pipe. (The pipe is used as a chimney to vent excess smoke.)

Next, place an electric hot plate in the bottom of the smoker. This will be the sole source of heat. Procure an old cast-iron skillet to sit on top of the hot plate, and fill it with maple or hickory sawdust. Place the fish or meat to be smoked on the upper racks in the smoker. Keep the temperature at 200° or slightly lower. Additional sawdust may be required during smoking.

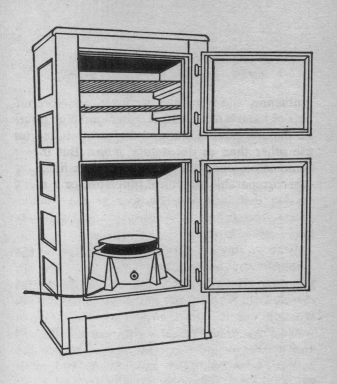

Smokehouses

Most devotees of smoked foods will not go so far as to build a permanent frame smokehouse. Although once an essential part of farm life all across the country, the traditional smokehouse is only feasible for people who have reason to process large quantities of meat.

A true smokehouse, a separate building made from wood, brick, or stone, should be a minimum of fifty feet from any other building on the property. Smokehouses are relatively simple to build, but are designed so that they need careful supervision. (See diagram for materials required.)

Most smokehouses utilize an outside fire pit for easy temperature control and to reduce the danger of fire inside the house. Seams and ventilators should fit tightly for effective air flow.

To judge how much meat will fit at one time in a smokehouse, the USDA advises to allow twelve inches in width both ways and two feet in height for each piece of meat hung. Two or more rows can be hung at one time.

(See pages 190–92 for a list of commercial smokehouses, many of which sell their professionally smoked meats through the mail.)

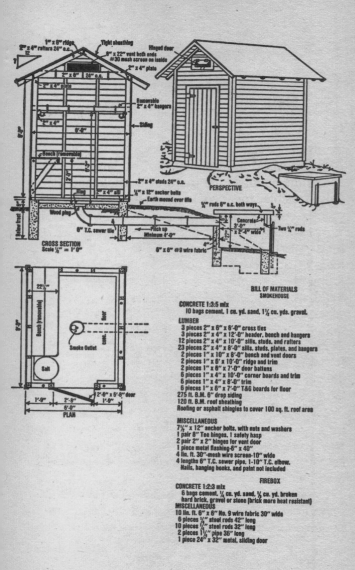

1" x 6" ridge
2" x 4" rafters 24" o.c.
Tight sheathing
Hinged door
8" x 22" vent both ends
#30 mesh screen on inside
2" x 4" plate
2" x 6"   24" o.c.
2" x 4" plate
Removable
2" x 4" hangers
2" x 4"
Siding
6'-0"
Bench (removable)
2" x 4" studs 24" o.c.
Ring
2" x 4" sill
Earth mound over tile
7½" x 12" anchor bolts
Wood plug
Below frost line
6" T.C. sewer tile
Pitch up
Minimum 4'-0"
6" x 6" #9 wire fabric
½" rods 6" o.c. both ways
Concrete
2" x 4" wide
Two ½" rods

CROSS SECTION
Scale ¼" = 1'0"

PERSPECTIVE

PLAN

22½"
Bench (removable)
Conc. floor
Smoke Outlet
Salt
2'-6" x 6'-8" door
1'-9"   **2'-8"**   **1'-9"**
6'-0"

BILL OF MATERIALS
SMOKEHOUSE

CONCRETE 1:3:5 mix
 10 bags cement, 1 cu. yd. sand, 1½ cu. yds. gravel.

LUMBER
 3 pieces 2" x 6" x 6'-0" cross ties
 3 pieces 2" x 4" x 12'-0" header, bench and hangers
 12 pieces 2" x 4" x 10'-0" sills, studs, and rafters
 23 pieces 2" x 4" x 8'-0" sills, studs, plates, and hangers
 2 pieces 1" x 10" x 8'-0" bench and vent doors
 2 pieces 1" x 6" x 10'-0" ridge and trim
 2 pieces 1" x 6" x 7'-0" door battens
 6 pieces 1" x 4" x 10'-0" corner boards and trim
 6 pieces 1" x 4" x 8'-0" trim
 6 pieces 1" x 6" x 7'-0" T&G boards for floor
 275 ft. B.M. 6" drop siding
 120 ft. B.M. roof sheathing
 Roofing or asphalt shingles to cover 100 sq. ft. roof area

MISCELLANEOUS
 7½" x 12" anchor bolts, with nuts and washers
 1 pair 8" Tee hinges, 1 safety hasp
 2 pair 2" x 2" hinges for vent door
 1 piece metal flashing–6" x 40"
 4 lin. ft. 30"–mesh wire screen–10" wide
 4 lengths 6" T.C. sewer pipe, 1-10" T.C. elbow.
 Nails, hanging hooks, and paint not included

FIREBOX
CONCRETE 1:2:3 mix
 6 bags cement, ¼ cu. yd. sand, ½ cu. yd. broken
 hard brick, gravel or stone (brick more heat resistant)
MISCELLANEOUS
 10 lin. ft. 6" x 6" No. 9 wire fabric 30" wide
 6 pieces ¼" steel rods 42" long
 10 pieces ¼" steel rods 32" long
 2 pieces 1½" pipe 36" long
 1 piece 24" x 32" metal, sliding door

35

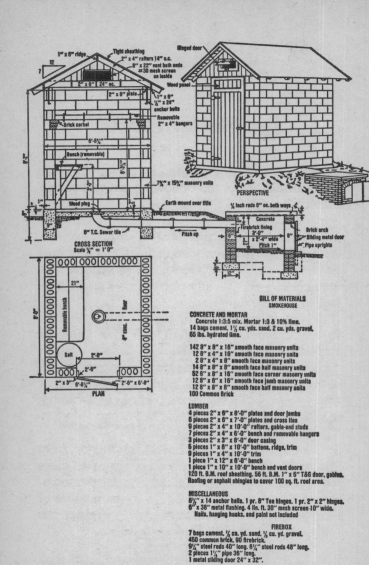

Tight sheathing

1" x 6" ridge

2" x 4" rafters 14" o.c.

8" x 22" vent both ends
#30 mesh screen
on inside

Hinged door

Wood panel

7 / 12

2" x 6" 24" o.c.

2" x 6" plate

1" x 6"
½" x 24"
anchor bolts

Removable
2" x 4" hangers

Brick corbel

6'-8½"

Bench (removable)

6'-8½"

8'-2"

7½" x 15½" masonry units

Wood plug

Earth mound over tile

½ inch rods 8" o.c. both ways

Concrete

Firebrick lining
3'-0"

Brick arch

9"

6" T.C. Sewer tile

Pitch up

x 2'-6" wide
Pitch 1"

8"

Sliding metal door

Pipe uprights

9"

12"

CROSS SECTION
Scale ¼" = 1' 0"

PERSPECTIVE

21"

Removable bench

8'-0"

4" conc. floor

Salt

2'-8"

2'-6"

2" x 3"

6'-8½"

2'-6" x 6'-8"

PLAN

Courtesy of U.S. Department of Agriculture

36

For Best Results

Whichever kind of smokehouse you decide to try for yourself, keep the following suggestions in mind:

1. Smokehouses should be well-contained systems with virtually no unplanned leaks or unnecessary places for smoke to escape, so the temperature and air and smoke flow can be controlled and regulated.

2. Regulation of smoke and air flow becomes critical to successful smoking. A rapid draft is necessary to start the smoking process and eliminate excess moisture; less rapid air movement at the end of the process keeps meat from shrinking in weight.

3. Standard smoking temperature ranges from 90° to 120°F. (This may not pertain in all cases to electric smoking appliances.) Use a thermometer to determine rises and falls in the amount of heat your fire is producing, and to register the temperature where the meat is hanging.

4. A smokehouse can accommodate more than one cut of meat at a time, but pieces should not

touch each other or come in contact with the smokehouse walls.

5. Cured meats absorb smoke more slowly than uncured cuts, and if exposed to too much smoke too suddenly, cuts can become discolored.

6. Different foods require different exposures to smoke. In general, allow several days for hams and large cuts; twelve hours to two days for sausage; eight to twelve hours for poultry; two to four hours for fish. Individual taste preferences and temperatures also affect the process. Experiment until you are satisfied with the end result.

Chapter 4.

Cures and Marinades

Cures or brines and marinades play an important role in smoke cookery. The former serve primarily to preserve food, but can also include ingredients for distinctive flavoring; the latter act as flavoring and tenderizing agents. Both will make a great difference in the quality and the taste of your smoked foods.

About Curing

Prior to smoking, large fresh cuts of meat should be carefully cured, both for taste and as an extra safeguard against contamination.

Curing with salt, still the most popular practice, dates back to the Mesolithic people who lived near the ocean and discovered the preservative properties in sea salt.

There are a number of accepted cures for meat, all using salt as their base. As the salt oxidizes, it kills bacteria that can cause the meat to spoil. Saltpeter, a chemical composed of potassium and nitric acid, is one kind of salt frequently used in curing.

As you prepare a cure, measure the ingredients precisely. Always base your figures on the exact weight of the meat: too little salt can cause decay; too much salt can produce a hard, dry product.

A general rule in curing with salt is to provide one tenth the weight of the meat in salt; one fortieth the weight of the salt for saltpeter.

As meats cure, they give off moisture and become dryer; some will lose as much as five pounds in the process. So be sure to use a large container (a crock or barrel) to allow for the liquid that will be added by the product itself.

Chill meat as it cures, and keep it cold (from 36° to 40°F.). Temperatures below 36°F. can retard the salt's absorption.

Salt cures are used in almost every case on fish and generally on pork. Hams and bacon can be flavored further by adding sugar or syrup, beer, vinegar, pepper, and wines to the basic recipes.

Smoked Salt

Make a shallow tray of heavy-duty aluminum foil to fit in the center of the cooking grill. Spread a very shallow layer of table salt on the foil tray, cover, and smoke for several hours, or until the salt is lightly colored and tastes smoky. Cool and store in a tightly covered container.

Use in cooking to add smoke flavor, or put in salt dish for seasoning at the table.

Courtesy of Smoke 'N Pit Corporation

Dry Cure for Pork

6-8 pounds salt
2 pounds brown or white sugar
2 ounces saltpeter

Mix ingredients thoroughly. Divide mixture into two equal parts, one to use immediately, one to set aside. Rub one part of the cure on the meat, poking some into ends and crevices. Pat it on the outside of cuts to a thickness of ⅛ inch.

Fit meat into a barrel or crock (not aluminum) without disturbing the salt coat. Keep it in a cool place. Hams and pork shoulders should be stored 2 days per pound; bacon 1½ days per pound.

In 6 to 8 days, remove meat, rinse it, and resalt it with the remaining portion of the cure.

Note: The above amount is adequate for 100 pounds of ham or pork shoulder; make half this amount for bacon and smaller cuts.

Courtesy of U.S. Department of Agriculture

Sweet Pickle Cure for Pork

8 pounds salt
2 pounds brown or white sugar
2 ounces saltpeter
4½ gallons water

Dissolve dry ingredients in water 36° to 40° F. Fit chilled cuts into clean barrel or crock and cover with cold solution. Place a weight on the meat to keep it from floating. Store in a cold place.

On the seventh day, remove the meat, pour out the cure solution (reserve it and stir it), repack the meat, and cover it again with the cure. Repeat this process on the fourteenth and twenty-eighth days.

If the cure becomes sour or syrupy, throw it away and make a new batch.

For total curing time, allow 3½ to 4 days per pound for hams and shoulders, and a minimum of 28 days for smaller cuts.

Courtesy of U.S. Department of Agriculture

Cure for Fish

This recipe can be used with cod, bass, pike, tuna, sturgeon, mackerel, eel, squid, and octopus.

2 quarts water
1 cup noniodized salt
½ cup brown sugar
2 tablespoons lemon concentrate or **¼** cup lemon
    juice
¼ tablespoon garlic powder
¼ tablespoon onion powder

Mix ingredients and stir until dissolved. Cover small fish or fillets of large fish for 4 hours or more. Rinse, dry, and load into smoker. Keep in smoker for 4 to 10 hours, depending on the size of the pieces.

Courtesy of Luhr Jensen and Sons, Inc.

About Marinades

The word "marinade," a derivative of *mare*, the Latin word for sea, was originally applied to simple brines for fish. Today, most marinades include an oil and an acid, which take on the flavor of other ingredients in the recipe and in turn permeate the food soaked in them.

You can marinate the tougher cuts of meat to tenderize them, or soak the best cuts simply to flavor them. Use containers that are ample enough to allow the food to be totally or almost totally covered. If the food is turned several times, it need not be completely submerged.

Avoid aluminum bowls, which can discolor

and taint the food. Instead, use glass, stainless steel, or glazed pottery. A heavy-duty plastic bag will work as well.

The length of time required to marinate foods varies and is up to individual experimentation. Foods that are left to marinate at room temperature are ready to cook sooner, but are also susceptible to faster spoilage. With most of the recipes given on the following pages, you can let foods marinate overnight, covered, in the refrigerator.

As a general rule, if you don't want to wait this long, allow 2 to 4 hours for chicken, fish, and other kinds of seafood; 4 to 6 hours for diced or small cuts of meat; and overnight for large, whole cuts and birds.

If you are pressed for time and don't want to make your own marinade from scratch, try bottled marinades from a grocery store. Barbecue sauce, pineapple juice, cider, apricot nectar, soy sauce, and teriyaki sauce will all work as flavoring marinades for many kinds of foods.

After the food has been adequately marinated, remove it and pat it dry. Save the marinade to make a sauce, or to baste the food as it cooks.

Barbecued Chicken Marinade

½ cup soy sauce
½ cup pineapple juice
¼ cup cooking oil
1 teaspoon dry mustard
1 tablespoon brown sugar
2 teaspoons ground ginger
1 teaspoon garlic salt
¼ teaspoon pepper

Combine ingredients in a small saucepan. Simmer for 5 minutes; let cool. Marinate chicken for at least one hour. Use remaining sauce to baste during cooking.

Courtesy of La Choy Food Products

Barbecued Shrimp Marinade

⅓ cup soy sauce
⅓ cup salad oil
⅓ cup sherry
½ teaspoon onion powder
¼ teaspoon ground ginger

Combine ingredients. Pour over shrimp in shallow glass baking dish. Cover and refrigerate. Reserve marinade to use as basting sauce during cooking.

Courtesy of La Choy Food Products

Basic Beef Marinade

½ cup water
½ cup red wine
4 peppercorns, crushed
1 bay leaf
1 teaspoon powdered cloves
1 onion, chopped
½ teaspoon powdered mustard

Combine all ingredients in a bowl. Let beef sit in liquid overnight.

Beer Marinade

1 cup beer
½ cup oil
1 onion, chopped
1 clove garlic, crushed

Combine ingredients and stir until well mixed. Use with beef or shrimp.

Chicken Marinade

8 ounces French dressing
1 teaspoon garlic powder
1 tablespoon oregano
1 teaspoon salt
1 cup white wine

Mix above ingredients, and heat, stirring slowly. Use as marinade and as basting sauce with chicken.

Courtesy of W. C. Bradley Co.

Cider Marinade for Ham

1 quart cider
½ cup raisins
1 teaspoon allspice

Mix other ingredients and pour over ham which has been stuck with 10 to 20 cloves. Refrigerate overnight, turning ham several times. Reserve some of the marinade and cook ham in it, or baste it during cooking.

Creole Beef Marinade

¼ cup oil
¼ cup bourbon or sherry
2 tablespoons soy sauce
1 teaspoon Worcestershire sauce
1 teaspoon garlic powder
Pepper to taste

Mix ingredients well. Add meat and marinate at least 12 hours in refrigerator.

Courtesy of Luhr Jensen and Sons, Inc.

Fruit Marinade for Pork

1 cup apricot or pear nectar
1 can (8¼ ounces) crushed pineapple
½ cup catsup
¼ cup brown sugar
2 tablespoons vinegar
1 teaspoon salt
½ teaspoon garlic powder
½ teaspoon lemon pepper

Combine all ingredients. Use with ribs, chops, roasts, or fresh ham.

Courtesy of The Brinkmann Corporation

Gourmet's Delight Marinade

½ cup fine olive oil
1 cup chopped carrots
1 cup chopped parsley
¼ cup chopped chives
5 cloves garlic, crushed
2 bay leaves
6 cups water
6 cups red wine
6 cups vinegar
1 tablespoon allspice
Salt and pepper to taste

Heat oil in skillet and add carrots, parsley, chives, and garlic. Cook slowly without browning, until all ingredients are soft but still retain their color. Add all other ingredients and simmer covered, for an hour.

Let marinade cool slightly, adjust seasonings, and strain through fine sieve or cheesecloth.

Lemon-Ginger Basting Sauce

1 can frozen lemonade (undiluted)
¼ teaspoon ground ginger
Salt and pepper to taste

Combine above ingredients and mix well. Pour over chicken and refrigerate for several hours. Reserve sauce and baste with it during cooking.

Courtesy of Charcoal Briquet Institute

Lemon-Herb Marinade

⅓ cup lemon juice
¼ cup salad oil
2 tablespoons water
½ teaspoon celery salt
1 clove garlic, crushed
½ teaspoon salt
¼ teaspoon dried marjoram
¼ teaspoon dried rosemary
¼ teaspoon dried thyme
1 small onion, peeled and grated
½ teaspoon pepper

Combine ingredients in jar with tight-fitting lid. Shake well. Use as marinade and as basting sauce during cooking.

Courtesy of W. C. Bradley Co.

Maple-Flavored Turkey Marinade

½ cup salt
⅓ cup brown sugar
½ teaspoon maple flavoring
1 teaspoon onion powder
1 teaspoon celery salt
1 bay leaf, crushed
1 cup dry white wine
1 tablespoon pepper
3 cups water

Mix ingredients and soak turkey for 8 to 12 hours. Remove from marinade, rinse, and air-dry. Place on rack in smoker and smoke for 30 minutes per pound. Remove from smoker and bake in oven at 300°F. allowing approximately 15 minutes per pound.

Courtesy of Luhr Jensen and Sons, Inc.

Marinade Sauce

1½ cups oil
¾ cup soy sauce
¼ cup Worcestershire sauce
2 tablespoons dry mustard
¼ teaspoon salt
½ cup wine vinegar
1½ teaspoons parsley flakes
2 cloves garlic, crushed
⅓ cup lemon juice

Combine all ingredients and mix well. Cover steaks, lamb chops, or other small cuts with the marinade and chill for at least several hours before cooking.

Courtesy of Metals Engineering Corporation

Milk Marinade for Fish

2 cups milk
Salt and pepper to taste

Prior to cooking any kind of white fish, soak it for an hour in milk that has had a little salt and pepper added. The fish will stay moist and tender as a result.

Oriental Marinade for Pork

⅓ cup lemon juice
¼ cup sherry
¼ cup soy sauce
¼ cup vinegar
¼ cup honey
3 tablespoons brown sugar
2 teaspoons Worcestershire sauce
½ teaspoon ground ginger
½ teaspoon garlic powder

Combine all ingredients. Use with chops, roasts, ribs, and steaks.

Courtesy of The Brinkmann Corporation

Oriental Marinade for Steak

½ cup soy sauce
1 tablespoon sesame seeds
¼ cup sake or dry white wine
1 onion, chopped
½ cup chopped green pepper
1 clove garlic, crushed
½ teaspoon ginger

Blend ingredients and pour over steak. Marinate overnight. When ready to cook, remove steak from marinade, brush with oil. Reserve marinade and baste steak several times as it cooks. Heat remaining marinade and serve as sauce with cooked steaks.

Courtesy of Charmglow Products

Patio Chicken Marinade

1 cup oil
⅓ cup lemon juice
3 tablespoons soy sauce
1 clove garlic, crushed
1 teaspoon oregano
1 teaspoon MSG (optional)
½ teaspoon salt
¼ teaspoon pepper

Combine ingredients, pour over chicken, and refrigerate for 4 to 5 hours, turning occasionally. Baste with marinade during cooking.

Courtesy of Turco Manufacturing Company

Quick Onion Marinade

1 can or package onion soup
1 cup water or white wine
Salt and pepper to taste

Open a package or a can of onion soup and simmer it slowly with the liquid. Correct the seasoning to taste, and pour over poultry or beef.

Rib Marinade

Sprinkle lemon juice and seasoned pepper on ribs and refrigerate them overnight or for at least 3 hours. Before cooking, rub with peanut oil. Paint with barbecue sauce before or after cooking.

Courtesy of Bosman Industries, Inc.

Savory Sirloin Marinade

2 tablespoons oil
1 cup chili sauce
¼ cup catsup
¼ cup hot sauce
2 cloves garlic, crushed
1 cup dry red wine
1 tablespoon brown sugar
2 tablespoons honey
2 teaspoons dry mustard

Combine ingredients and pour over meat. Marinate at least one hour. Drain well, and reserve marinade to baste meat as it cooks.

Courtesy of Charmglow Products

Sayonara Marinade

An excellent seasoning for chicken wings! Combine equal parts of soy sauce, sherry, and oil.

Pour over chicken wings, season to taste with garlic powder and ground ginger. Marinate for at least one hour and drain.

Courtesy of Charcoal Briquet Institute

Shish Kebab Marinade

2 medium onions, thinly sliced
½ cup wine or wine vinegar
¼ cup salad oil
1 teaspoon oregano
Salt and pepper
Garlic to taste

Combine all ingredients in a large bowl. Add beef or lamb chunks and refrigerate overnight.

Courtesy of W. C. Bradley Co.

Simple Marinade for Fish

White wine
Soy sauce
Oil

Depending on the size of the fish you plan to cook, combine equal portions of the above 3 ingredients. Turn fish frequently to allow marinade to flavor each side equally.

Courtesy of W. C. Bradley Co.

Simple Marinade for Poultry I

8 ounces Russian, Italian, or French salad
   dressing
⅓ cup oil
Salt and pepper to taste

Season chicken with salt and pepper. Place
pieces in a large bowl and pour desired dressing
and oil over them. Turn pieces until they are
well coated. Chill for at least 2 hours or overnight. Drain, and reserve sauce for occasional
basting during cooking.

Courtesy of Charcoal Briquet Institute

Simple Marinade for Poultry II

1 cup oil
1 cup vermouth

This mixture gives chicken or duck a moist,
tangy flavor. Combine the liquids in a bowl and
soak poultry for several hours, or overnight, in
the refrigerator, turning and basting several
times.

Courtesy of W. C. Bradley Co.

Smoker Special Marinade

1 cup water
½ cup sherry
½ cup soy sauce
2 cloves garlic, crushed
½ cup honey

Although any marinade will work well with smoked foods, this one is particularly piquant for beef or chicken. Combine all ingredients and allow meat to stand in them for at least 12 hours. Stir occasionally to keep honey from settling to the bottom.

Courtesy of W. C. Bradley Co.

Spicy Tomato Marinade

4 cups peeled, seeded, chopped tomatoes
3 tablespoons white vinegar
2 teaspoons Worcestershire sauce
3 ounces lemon juice
1 tablespoon sugar
1½ teaspoons mustard
¼ teaspoon dried thyme, marjoram, or basil
Salt and pepper to taste

Combine above ingredients and simmer for several hours; add some water to keep it from thickening. Correct seasonings. Watch carefully to make sure it does not scorch the bottom of the pan while cooking. Use with poultry or beef.

This recipe provides an excellent way to use up an abundance of tomatoes from an overflowing garden, and the marinade freezes very nicely.

Tangerine Marinade for Poultry

1 can frozen tangerine juice
1 cup water
½ cup white wine or dry vermouth

Mix above ingredients in a large bowl. Add split chicken breasts, wings, or other chicken white meat. Refrigerate for several hours or overnight, and baste with juice during cooking.

Teriyaki Marinade

¾ cup pineapple juice
2 tablespoons soy sauce
2 tablespoons lemon juice
2 cloves garlic, crushed
1 small bay leaf
⅛ teaspoon ground cloves

Combine pineapple juice and remaining ingredients in pint-sized screw-top jar. Cover and shake well. Refrigerate until ready to use. Recommended with top sirloin for maximum flavor. Reserve sauce after marinating to baste meat during cooking.

Courtesy of W. C. Bradley Co.

Wine Marinade for Pork

1 cup red wine
¼ cup lemon juice
¼ cup oil
2 tablespoons steak sauce
Dash hot pepper sauce
2 cloves garlic, crushed

Combine all ingredients and use to marinate pork roast. Poke roast with long two-tined fork in several places so marinade can penetrate meat.

Courtesy of The Brinkmann Corporation

RECIPES

APPETIZERS

Chicken Liver Kebabs

Cut chicken livers to desired size. Dry on absorbent paper toweling. Thread a piece of liver, a square of bacon, and a mushroom cap on a skewer and repeat until skewers are filled. Paint with oil and roll in bread crumbs. Lay skewers on grill and smoke about 45 minutes.

Courtesy of Bosman Industries, Inc.

Clam Dip

1 pint sour cream
1 envelope prepared spaghetti sauce mix
¾ cup sautéed minced smoked clams

Combine all ingredients and refrigerate for one hour. Serve with potato chips or crackers. *(Makes about 2 cups.)*

Courtesy of R. T. French Company

Smoky Clam Dip

8 ounces cream cheese
1 can (6½ ounces) minced smoked clams
Dash Worcestershire sauce
Dash lemon juice
Salt and pepper to taste
⅛ teaspoon garlic powder

Smoke clams for 15 to 20 minutes on an oiled screen using apple or alder chips, if available. Mix clams with other ingredients and chill before serving.

Courtesy of Luhr Jensen and Sons, Inc.

Date Tidbits

Wrap a thin slice of cheese around a pitted date and cover with a thin slice of boiled ham. Brush lightly with butter and grill until lightly browned over gray coals. Serve with red wine heated with orange or lemon juice, and whole spices such as cloves, cinnamon sticks, nutmeg, and allspice.

Courtesy of Charcoal Briquet Institute

Char-Grilled Grapefruit

3 grapefruit
½ cup firmly packed brown sugar
⅓ cup soft butter or margarine
½ cup dark rum (optional)

Cut grapefruit into halves. Cut a thin slice from bottom of each half to allow them to stand straight. Loosen sections with a sharp knife or grapefruit spoon. In a bowl, mix sugar, butter, and rum. Spread sugar mixture thickly on top of grapefruit. Place them sugar side up on grill 6 inches above medium coals. Grill for 10 to 12 minutes, without turning, until top of grapefruit swells slightly and is hot to the touch. Serve while still hot.

Courtesy of Charcoal Briquet Institute

Honey Barbecued Pineapple Wedges

1 fresh pineapple, unpared
¾ cup honey
¼ cup melted butter

Cut pineapple into 6 long wedges, leaving top of pineapple attached to provide a handle for turning wedges on grill. Remove core from pineapple wedges; mix honey and butter and brush over pineapple. Place wedges on grill 6 inches above medium coals, turning several times until lightly browned. Grill about 10 to 12 minutes, brushing wedges occasionally with honey mixture. (If fresh pineapple is not available, canned pineapple slices can be prepared in the same way after they have been well drained. Grill them only 4 to 5 minutes.)

Courtesy of Charcoal Briquet Institute

Mushroom Dip

4 ounces cream cheese
2 tablespoons chopped canned or cooked fresh mushrooms
4 tablespoons mushroom liquid
1½ tablespoons chopped smoked beef
½ teaspoon chopped parsley
1 drop Tabasco sauce

Mix cheese softened at room temperature with the mushroom liquid and then add remaining ingredients. Use as a dip with crackers or to stuff celery.

Nuts and Chex Snacks

¼ cup salad oil
1 cup smoked nuts
4 cups Chex breakfast cereal (wheat, corn, or rice)
1 envelope dry prepared chili mix

Heat oil in large skillet. Add nuts and cereal, stirring to coat with oil. Add contents of chili mix, carefully stirring to coat all pieces evenly. Place over cooler coals (or low oven heat) and cook slowly, stirring constantly, for about 5 to 10 minutes. Cool before serving.

Courtesy of R. T. French Company

Party Cheese Ball

4 ounces Cheddar cheese, grated
1 8-ounce package cream cheese
1 3-ounce wedge Roquefort cheese (optional)
½ teaspoon Liquid Smoke
Chopped parsley or chopped pecans

Mix all ingredients except parsley and pecans, and shape into a ball. Roll in parsley or pecans. Chill and serve with assorted crackers.

Courtesy of E. H. Wright Company, Inc.

Salmon Party Log

1 pound can of salmon
1 8-ounce package cream cheese, softened
1 teaspoon prepared horseradish
¼ teaspoon Liquid Smoke
1 tablespoon lemon juice
2 teaspoons finely chopped onion
¼ teaspoon salt
½ cup chopped pecans
3 tablespoons fresh parsley

Drain and flake salmon, removing skin and bone. Combine salmon with remaining ingredients. Combine chopped pecans and parsley. Shape salmon mixture in 8x2-inch log. Roll in nut mixture and chill well.

Courtesy of E. H. Wright Company, Inc.

Sayonara Chicken Wings

Place chicken wings in equal parts of soy sauce, sherry, and oil. Season to taste with garlic powder and ground ginger. Marinate for one hour, then drain and spear. Grill 6 inches from gray coals until cooked and golden brown. Turn during cooking to permit even browning.

Courtesy of Charcoal Briquet Institute

Smoked Beef Rolls

Mix one package of cream cheese, a dash of Worcestershire sauce, and ½ teaspoon sharp mustard until smooth. Spread this on flat smoked beef slices and roll up snugly. Cut into halves and refrigerate. Serve as an appetizer or as a salad accompaniment.

Courtesy of Mrs. C. H. Crugan/McArthur's Smokehouse

Smoked Cheese I

Cheddar, Monterey Jack, Swiss, beer cheese, and other hard varieties can be smoked if kept a great distance from the heat of the fire. These are best smoked in electric smokers, or apparatus where you can control the distance of the food to the smoke.

Section cheese into cubes approximately 1½ inches thick. Place on wire grills or hardware cloth and smoke about 50 minutes. Cover and allow cubes to sit for an hour at room temperature before serving.

Courtesy of Luhr Jensen and Sons, Inc.

Smoked Cheese II

Use an 8-ounce package of cream cheese, or a block of any other cheese such as Monterey

Jack, Muenster, Cheddar. Cheese should be a fairly flat rectangle, shaped much like the cream cheese, and not more than one inch thick. Put one or several pieces of cheese on a piece of foil and put on cooking grill. Cover and smoke flavor and hour or two. Take cheese out if it begins to melt. Serve while warm to spread on crackers or with fruit for dessert. Or cool, then wrap well and chill until ready to serve.

Courtesy of Smoke 'N Pit Corporation

Smoked Eggs

Hard-boil and peel eggs. Arrange on cooking grill and smoke flavor for half an hour. Wrap in plastic wrap or close in plastic bag and chill for snacks.

Courtesy of Smoke 'N Pit Corporation

Smoked Lamb Canapés

Slice smoked leg of lamb into thin pieces. Place on rounds of dark raisin bread and add a dab of chutney or ginger marmalade to each. Serve as appetizers.

Courtesy of Mrs. George Bliss/McArthur's Smokehouse

Smoked Liver Pâté

1 pound smoked chicken liver
½ pound sliced bacon
1 large onion
4 cloves garlic
4 bay leaves
1 teaspoon salt
¼ teaspoon red pepper
2 tablespoons steak sauce
½ teaspoon nutmeg
1 teaspoon mustard
⅛ teaspoon ground cloves

Put liver in covered pan with cut-up bacon. Add bay leaves, onion, garlic, salt, pepper, and steak sauce. Bring this to a boil and cook for 20 minutes in just enough water to cover. When done, discard bay leaves. Add remaining ingredients and put in blender, then into molds. This will keep in the refrigerator for a week and it will also freeze well.

Courtesy of Luhr Jensen and Sons, Inc.

Smoked Nuts

Many different kinds of nuts can become more flavorful when smoked. Almonds, walnuts, peanuts, cashews, Brazil nuts, chestnuts, canned mixed nuts, and sunflower and pumpkin seeds are among those you can experiment with.

Spread nuts on fine screen or on aluminum foil pierced with many holes. Smoke for not more than one hour with your favorite flavor fuel. (Like cheese, nuts will take on a burned flavor if exposed to too much smoke.)

To salt the nuts before smoking, soak nuts for a few minutes in a light saline solution. Drain and then smoke.

For a saltier taste, apply fine salt by shaking smoked nuts and salt in a plastic bag after smoking.

Courtesy of Luhr Jensen and Sons, Inc.

Smoked Nuts

Make a shallow tray of heavy-duty aluminum foil to fit on cooking grill. Spread whole plain or salted almonds, walnuts, cashews, filberts, pecans, or peanuts on foil tray. Smoke flavor for several hours. Cool, then store in tightly covered containers or plastic bags.

Courtesy of Smoke 'N Pit Corporation

Smoked Oysters

Drain fresh or canned oysters (allow 4 or 5 per person) and salt lightly. Wrap each one in a slice of bacon and fasten ends of bacon together with wooden toothpicks. Smoke slowly, 4 to 6 inches from heat, turning once or twice. Oysters are ready when bacon is crispy and sizzling. Serve while still warm.

Smoked Popcorn

This is an unusual recipe, but it really works! Smoke flavor 1 cup of popcorn (unpopped) for 30 minutes. If available, use a mixture of apple and cherry chips. Place smoked kernels in a mason jar and add 2 tablespoons of cranberry, pineapple, orange, or other fruit juices for each cup of smoked corn. Seal for one week. (The liquid replaces the moisture the corn lost during smoking.) Pop in the normal manner and add butter and salt to taste.

The same process will also work with wild rice.

Courtesy of Luhr Jensen and Sons, Inc.

Smoked Shrimp

Fresh shrimp tastes best in this recipe, but frozen shrimp will suffice. Peel and remove veins from shrimp and spread them on aluminum foil, or a grill with tight enough mesh to keep them from falling through. Brush liberally with tomato sauce or prepared barbecue sauce and smoke over hot coals for 2 to 4 minutes, basting with additional sauce.

Smoked Shrimp or Crayfish

Prepare a foil pan made from large pieces of heavy-duty aluminum foil at least ½ inch deep. Place ½ cup butter, 2 cloves of crushed garlic, and Tabasco in foil pan and set on grill. Add 3 pounds shelled, deveined shrimp or crayfish, 1 large green pepper cut in rings, 1 tablespoon minced onions, 1 teaspoon salt, and juice of 1 lemon. Mix well. Smoke for 45 minutes.

Courtesy of Bosman Industries, Inc.

Sailor's Shrimp

Peel and devein 1 pound of large, fresh shrimp and let stand overnight in marinade of your choice. Drain, reserving marinade, and cook over hot coals for 6 to 8 minutes, turning and basting frequently with remaining marinade.

Mariner's Shrimp or Lobster

⅔ cup vinegar
⅓ cup oil
1 envelope Sloppy Joe mix
1 pound cooked smoked shrimp or lobster

Combine vinegar, oil, and contents of sauce mix in a mixing bowl. Blend well. Pour over shrimp or chunks of lobster. Cover and refrigerate several hours. Serve as an hors d'oeuvre on crackers.

Courtesy of R. T. French Company

Smoky Shrimp Cocktail

Spread fresh cooked or canned shrimp on oiled screen and smoke for 25 minutes with hickory fuel. Serve chilled in cocktail sauce or heated in your favorite chili sauce.

Courtesy of Luhr Jensen and Sons, Inc.

Smoky Salmon on Celery Sticks

1 cup smoked flaked salmon
1 3-ounce package cream cheese
2 tablespoons mayonnaise
Salt to taste
6 stalks crisp celery

Mix salmon with next 3 ingredients. Pack grooves of celery with mixture and cut into ¾-inch pieces.

Courtesy of Luhr Jensen and Sons, Inc.

Stryker's Strike

This recipe is especially suited for serving as a dip or on toast.

1 cup cottage cheese
2 teaspoons minced parsley or chives
2 teaspoons white horseradish
4 green stuffed olives, chopped
Dash paprika
½ pound chipped beef

Combine all ingredients, stirring thoroughly, and add enough light cream to moisten to desired consistency. Serve on melba toast.

Courtesy of David Stryker/McArthur's Smokehouse

Stuffed Mushrooms

1 pound fresh mushrooms with large caps
4 tablespoons butter
½ cup dry white wine
3 tablespoons chopped onion
¾ cup dry bread crumbs
2 teaspoons sage
Salt and pepper to taste

Slice stems off mushrooms, keeping caps intact. Melt 3 tablespoons of butter in a saucepan. Add the wine, bring to a boil, and add the mushroom caps, top down. Cook slowly for 4 minutes.

Chop remaining stems into small pieces. In a separate saucepan melt remaining butter. Sauté onions until they are golden but not browned. Add pieces of mushroom stems and cook one minute longer. Remove from heat and stir in bread crumbs and seasonings.

Drain caps. Place on a flat surface, "dish" side down, and heap with stuffing. Cover with inverted cap, and press slightly so edges touch. (The finished product should slightly resemble a flying saucer.) Repeat procedure for remaining caps and thread closely together on skewers. Cook over hot coals for 2 to 4 minutes basting with butter.

Zippy Snack

1 tablespoon mayonnaise
½ pound smoked beef, chopped and shredded
3 ounces horseradish

Mix ingredients and serve on toast. If desired, use ½ cup mayonnaise or half mayonnaise and half cream cheese to make a dip.

Courtesy of Ruth Odebrecht/McArthur's Smokehouse

MEATS

GUIDE TO SMOKE COOKING MEAT ON A GRILL

When cooking large cuts of meat, degree of doneness may be accurately determined by use of a meat thermometer. Insert thermometer so that the bulb reaches the thickest part of the lean meat. Be sure it does not touch fat or bone. Follow directions with meat thermometer.

Food	Setting for Electric Smokers	Setting for Gas Smokers	Approx. Cooking Time	Special Instructions
BEEF Brisket—5 lb.	3	Low Flame	4½ to 5 hr.	Grill with hood down.
Hamburgers—½ inch thick	High	Medium to High Flame	8 to 15 min.	Season. Grill, turning once.
Roasts—4 to 6 lb. Rolled Rib Rare (140°)	4	Low Flame	1 hr. 30 min. to 2 hr. 30 min.	Place in shallow pan or grid. Cook with hood down. Use meat thermometer.
Medium (160°)	4	Low Flame	2 to 3 hr.	Same as above.
Well Done (170°)	4	Low Flame	2 hr. 45 min. to 3 hr. 30 min.	Same as above.

80

Rump, Sirloin Tip, Top Round (choice), Rolled and Tied

Rare (140°)	4	Low Flame	1 hr. 15 min. to 1 hr. 45 min.	Place in shallow pan on grid. Cook with hood down. Use meat thermometer.
Medium (160°)	4	Low Flame	1 hr. 30 min. to 2 hr.	Same as above.
Well Done (170°)	4	Low Flame	1 hr. 45 min. to 2 hr. 30 min.	Same as above.

STEAKS

Chuck (blade),* Club, Filet Mignon, Porterhouse, Rib, Sirloin Strip, T-Bone—1 inch thick

Rare	High	High Flame	8 to 12 min.	Remove excess fat from edge. Slash remaining fat at 2-inch intervals. Grill, turning once. Season each side as completed.
Medium	5	Medium to High Flame	12 to 20 min.	Same as above.
Well Done	4	Medium Flame	20 to 30 min.	Same as above.

1½ inches thick

Rare	High	High Flame	11 to 16 min.	Same as above.

*Use unseasoned meat tenderizer, following label instructions.

Food	Setting for Electric Smokers	Setting for Gas Smokers	Approx. Cooking Time	Special Instructions
Medium	5	Medium to High Flame	16 to 25 min.	Same as above.
Well Done	4	Medium Flame	25 to 35 min.	Same as above.
LAMB Chops and Steaks 1 inch thick				
Rare	High	High Flame	12 to 15 min.	Remove excess fat from edge. Slash remaining fat at 2-inch intervals. Grill, turning once. Season each side as completed.
Medium	5	Medium to High Flame	15 to 20 min.	Same as above.
Well Done	4	Medium Flame	20 to 30 min.	Same as above.
1½ inches thick Rare	High	High Flame	14 to 18 min.	Same as above.
Medium	5	Medium to High Flame	18 to 25 min.	Same as above.
Well Done	4	Medium Flame	25 to 35 min.	Same as above.

PORK (cook well done)				
Chops				
½ inch thick	5	Medium Flame	20 to 40 min.	Remove excess fat from edge. Slash remaining fat at 2-inch intervals. Season. Grill, turning frequently and moving if necessary.
1 inch thick	4	Medium Flame	35 to 60 min.	Same as above.
Ham (ready-to-eat)				
Steaks ½ inch thick	High	High Flame	12 to 15 min.	Remove excess fat from edge. Slash remaining fat at 2-inch intervals. Grill, turning once.
Whole 6 to 12 lb.	4	Low Flame	1 hr. 45 min. to 3 hr.	Place in shallow pan on grid. Cook with hood down. Use meat thermometer.
Ribs (barbecue)	2	Medium Flame	45 to 60 min.	Season. Grill, turning occasionally. During last few minutes, brush with barbecue sauce, turning several times.
SKINLESS WIENERS	5	Medium to High Flame	5 to 10 min.	Grill, turning once.

83

Courtesy of Turco Manufacturing Company

GUIDE TO COOKING MEAT ON THE ROTISSERIE

Insert spit through center of meat. Check for balance by cradling ends of spit in hands and rotating. Fasten with holding forks.

Food	Setting for Electric Smokers	Setting for Gas Smokers	Approx. Cooking Time	Special Instructions
BEEF				
Roasts—4 to 6 lb.				
Rolled Rib				
Rare (140°)	3	Low to Medium Flame	2 to 3 hr.	Season.
Medium (160°)	3	Low to Medium Flame	2 hr. 30 min. to 3 hr. 30 min.	Same as above.
Well Done (170°)	3	Low to Medium Flame	3 to 4 hr.	Same as above.
Rump, Sirloin Tip, Top Round (choice), Rolled and Tied	3 3 3			
Rare (140°)	3	Low to Medium Flame	1 hr. 30 min. to 2 hr. 15 min.	Season.

Medium (160°)	3	Low to Medium Flame	1 hr. 45 min. to 2 hr. 30 min.	Same as above.
Well Done (170°)	3	Low to Medium Flame	2 to 3 hr.	Same as above.
PORK (cook well done)				
Ribs (barbecue)	3	Low Flame	1 hr. to 1 hr. 30 min.	Season. Lace on spit. During last few minutes, brush with barbecue sauce.
Ham (ready-to-eat) 6 to 12 lb.	3	Low to Medium Flame	2 hr. to 3 hr. 30 min.	
Roasts—4 to 6 lb. Bone-In Loin (185°)	3	Low to Medium Flame	2 hr. 30 min. to 4 hr.	Season.
LAMB				
Leg—4 to 6 lb. Boned, rolled and tied Medium (175°)	3	Low to Medium Flame	2 hr. to 2 hr. 30 min.	Season.
Well Done (180°)	3	Low to Medium Flame	2 hr. 30 min. to 3 hr. 15 min.	Same as above.

85

Courtesy of Turco Manufacturing Company

COOKING CHART

CHARCOAL-WATER SMOKERS

Meat	Weight*	Charcoal	Wood	Water	Cooking Time
	3-4 lbs.	5 lbs.	2 sticks	4 qt.	3-4 hrs.
Beef	5-7 lbs.	7 lbs.	2 sticks	5 qt.	5-7 hrs.
Roast	8-10 lbs.	7 lbs.	3 sticks	6 qt.	7-8 hrs.
	11-13 lbs.	10 lbs.	3 sticks	7 qt.	8-9 hrs.
Pork	4-7 lbs.	7 lbs.	2 sticks	5 qt.	5-7 hrs.
Roast	8-10 lbs.	10 lbs.	3 sticks	6 qt.	7-9 hrs.
Pork Ribs	10 lbs.	8 lbs.	3 sticks	6 qt.	4-5 hrs.
Hams	5-10 lbs.	7 lbs.	2 sticks	4 qt.	4-5 hrs.
(pre-cooked)	15-20 lbs.	10 lbs.	4 sticks	7 qt.	6-8 hrs.
Hams	10 lbs.	10 lbs.	4 sticks	7 qt.	10-12 hrs.
Pork Chops	1" thick	6 lbs.	2 sticks	4 qt.	3-4 hrs.
Sausage Links	grill full	4 lbs.	1 stick	4 qt.	1½-2 hrs.
Lamb Roast	5-7 lbs.	7 lbs.	2 sticks	5 qt.	5-7 hrs.
Smoked Steaks	1½"-2" thick	7 lbs.	3 sticks	6 qt.	2-3 hrs.
Small Game	2½ lb. avg.	5 lbs.	2 sticks	5 qt.	4-5 hrs.
Large Game	8-12 lbs.	10-15	2 sticks	7 qt.	10-14 hrs.
Brisket	7 lb. avg.	7 lbs.	2 sticks	6 qt.	7 hrs.

General Rule: Hardwood briquettes will burn approximately 1 hour per lb.

Meats not listed will cook at the rate of approximately 1 hour per pound (minimum 5 lbs. hardwood briquettes)

Cooking time is determined by the largest single piece of meat being cooked.

Additional charcoal is not required for cooking on 2 or more levels.

*Weights given for each grill level.

Courtesy of Turco Manufacturing Company

Apricot Ham

1 fully-cooked boneless ham (about 5 pounds)
Whole cloves
1 cup apricot nectar
1 tablespoon brown sugar, firmly packed
1 tablespoon soy sauce
1 tablespoon lemon juice
1 tablespoon butter
1½ teaspoons ginger
1 teaspoon MSG
½ teaspoon curry powder
½ cup apricot preserves

Cut ham into ¼-inch slices; tie back together with sturdy string. Stud with cloves as you would a whole unsliced ham. Combine next 8 ingredients in saucepan. Bring to a boil; simmer 5 minutes. Cook ham on rotisserie spit over hot coals one hour, basting frequently with spicy apricot glaze. Combine remaining glaze and apricot preserves. Heat to boiling; simmer 2 minutes. Remove ham from rotisserie. Place ham on serving dish and carefully remove spit and string. Spread half of the apricot sauce over ham. Serve remaining sauce with ham. (10 servings)

Courtesy of Kikkoman International Inc.

Boneless Smoked Ham with Cumberland Fruit Sauce

7–10-pound fully cooked smoked ham
1 can (30 ounces) fruit cocktail
¼ cup frozen orange juice concentrate
¼ cup currant jelly
2 tablespoons sherry
¼ teaspoon ground ginger
2 tablespoons cornstarch
2 tablespoons lemon juice

Insert rotisserie rod lengthwise through center of ham (or place directly on grill). Balance ham and tighten spit forks so ham turns with rod. Insert meat thermometer at an angle so tip is in center of ham but not resting in fat or on rod. Place on rotisserie and cook at low to moderate temperature. To prepare sauce, drain fruit cocktail, reserve syrup, and set fruit aside; combine 1½ cups syrup with orange juice concentrate, jelly, sherry, and ginger in saucepan. Heat until jelly melts, stirring occasionally. Blend cornstarch and lemon juice until smooth and combine with jelly mixture. Cook, stirring occasionally, until mixture thickens. Brush ham with sauce during last 15 minutes cooking time.

Cook ham to 140°, allowing 15 to 18 minutes per pound. Add fruit cocktail to remaining sauce, heat for 1 to 2 minutes, and serve hot with ham. *(12–15 servings)*

Courtesy of National Livestock and Meat Board

Smoked Honey Ham

1 5-pound canned ham
Cloves
1 8-ounce can pineapple
1 12-ounce jar honey
½ cup brown sugar
1 jar cherries

This recipe is best suited for use on a water smoker grill, using a pan ¾ full of water to keep ham from drying out.

Place ham on grill above water. Place cloves and pineapple rings on surface of ham. Smoke on low temperature with hood closed for 60 minutes.

While ham is smoking, mix honey and brown sugar in double boiler and heat until easy to pour. Place cherries in center of pineapple rings. Pour honey mixture slowly over ham. Close hood and smoke another 30 minutes. *(10 servings)*

Courtesy of Charmglow Products

Banquet Feast

1 crown roast of smoked pork loin (9-12 pounds)
3 pounds sauerkraut
2 cups sauterne
1 pound loose sausage meat
1 package (12 ounces) prunes
Salt and pepper to taste
Dash garlic

Wash sauerkraut to remove salt. Simmer 2 hours in its own juice plus 2 cups sauterne. Add water if necessary. Fry sausage in small thumbnail-size pieces until brown. Cut prunes in ¼-inch pieces. Add sausage and prunes to sauerkraut.

Season crown roast with salt, pepper, and a dash of garlic. Place in shallow dish (a flat frying pan lid is perfect). Use aluminum foil as retaining dish. Fill center of crown roast with prune-sauerkraut stuffing. Cover center and bone tips with foil. Roast at 360°F. for about 2 hours. Serve with mashed potatoes, a green vegetable, and Cold Duck. Use juices from roast as gravy. *(6–10 servings)*

Courtesy of McArthur's Smokehouse

Barbecued Pork Chops

4 rib or loin pork chops, cut 1 inch thick
¾ cup tomato juice
¼ teaspoon hot red pepper sauce
¼ cup salad oil
2 tablespoons vinegar
¼ teaspoon Worcestershire sauce
⅛ teaspoon crushed basil
1 teaspoon brown bouquet sauce

Trim fat off chops and place in shallow pan. Combine next 6 ingredients and pour over chops. Let stand in refrigerator for 6 hours. Remove from marinade. Combine 2 tablespoons of marinade with bouquet sauce. Brush chops generously on both sides. Grill over medium setting for 15 minutes. Turn and continue grilling for 15 minutes more. *(4 servings)*

Courtesy of Turco Manufacturing Company

Smoky Barbecued Pork à la Worcestershire

1 cup catsup
½ cup water
¼ cup Worcestershire sauce
¼ cup salad oil
¼ cup white vinegar
1 tablespoon sugar
1 teaspoon onion powder
1 teaspoon salt
½ teaspoon hickory smoked salt
5-pound boneless top pork loin roast, tied for roasting

Prepare barbecue sauce by combining catsup, water, Worcestershire sauce, oil, vinegar, sugar, onion powder, salt, and smoked salt. Bring to boiling point; reduce heat and simmer uncovered for 30 minutes, stirring occasionally; set aside. Place pork on rack in a shallow open roasting pan. Insert meat thermometer into center of meat and roast in a preheated slow oven (325°F.) for 2 hours, or until thermometer registers 170°. Baste twice with barbecue sauce during last 30 minutes of roasting.

Remove pork (reserve drippings) to rack or

spit over hot coals. Brush with sauce. Grill over coals for 10 minutes, turning and brushing frequently with sauce. Mix reserved drippings with remaining sauce and ¼ cup water; reheat and serve in sauceboat along with roast. *(8 servings)*

Courtesy of Lee & Perrins

Game Sausage

This recipe will work for deer, reindeer, caribou, or moose.

10 pounds clean, fresh venison from trimmings and tough cuts
10 pounds pork
6 tablespoons salt
1 ounce (2 tablespoons) pepper
Pinch of sage

Grind meats and seasonings together thoroughly. Stuff into casings and smoke 8 to 10 hours at 110°F.

Courtesy of Cooperative Extension Service, University of Alaska

Note: Ask in your local grocery about casings, the intestines of pigs. They are standard items in Italian and German groceries, and can usually be obtained from any butcher shop that makes its own sausage. They are sold thoroughly cleaned but should be stored in salt if not used immediately.

Hunter's Delight Venison Sausage

2 tablespoons salt
2 teaspoons coarsly ground black pepper
¾ teaspoon mace
¼ teaspoon nutmeg
¼ teaspoon cloves
½ teaspoon allspice
½ teaspoon garlic powder
4 pounds boneless venison or beef, cut into 1½-inch cubes
4 pounds boneless pork butt or pork shoulder, cut into 1½-inch cubes

Sprinkle combined seasonings over meat cubes in a large bowl. Toss until well coated. Grind with desired grinding disc and stuff into casings. Smoke 8 to 10 hours.

Courtesy of Oster Corporation

Summer Sausage

10 pounds pork
15 pounds venison, reindeer, caribou, or moose
12 ounces salt
2 ounces pepper
2 ounces sugar

Grind pork and game meat finely. Add salt, pepper, and sugar. Mix very well, kneading like bread. Put into casings. Cold-smoke for 2 weeks.

Courtesy of Cooperative Extension Service, University of Alaska

General Tips for Cooking Beef Outdoors

Prepare enough beef to satisfy hearty outdoor appetites. For most groups allow the following amounts per person: ¼ to ½ pound ground beef; ½ pound boneless beef; ¾ to 1 pound beef with bone.

Cook all beef cuts at low to moderate temperatures. Meat cooked with high heat is less tender and juicy.

Keep a careful check on meat during cooking. Total time will vary with cut, weather, fire or heat, fuel, position on grill, and degree of doneness desired.

Use a meat thermometer to accurately determine doneness of large cuts of beef cooked on the rotisserie.

For flavor variety, brush beef with sauce or marinade during all or part of its cooking time. If the sauce is high in sugar or other ingredients that burn easily, it should be brushed on during the latter part of cooking time.

Use tongs rather than a fork to handle beef to prevent loss of flavorful juices.

Courtesy of National Live Stock and Meat Board

America's Favorite Steak

½ cup teriyaki sauce
1 teaspoon sugar
1 teaspoon lemon and pepper seasoning
½ teaspoon ginger
¼ teaspoon garlic salt
¼ teaspoon prepared mustard
2 beef T-bone or sirloin steaks, about 1 inch
  thick

Combine first 6 ingredients in shallow pan. Add steak, turning to coat both sides. Marinate at room temperature 20 minutes; turn over once. Remove steak; reserve marinade. Place on grill 4 to 5 inches from heat. Cook 8 to 10 minutes or until desired doneness. Brush occasionally with marinade. *(2–3 servings)*

Courtesy of Kikkoman International Inc.

Char-Broiled Flank Steak

1½ pounds flank steak
¼ cup Worcestershire sauce
⅓ cup soy sauce
1 teaspoon ground ginger or 1 teaspoon fresh
  ginger
Juice of 1 lemon

Place steak in shallow casserole dish and pour seasoning ingredients over it. Let marinate for a minimum of 3 hours, turning at least every hour. Grill above smoke for 3 to 4 minutes on each side. Slice diagonally. *(3–4 servings)*

Courtesy of Bosman Industries, Inc.

Coffee Citrus Round Steak

2 or 3 top round steaks, cut 1¼ inches thick
4 teaspoons freeze-dried or instant coffee
⅓ cup hot water
1 can (6 ounces) frozen orange juice concentrate, defrosted
2 tablespoons minced onion
1 tablespoon salt
1 tablespoon lemon juice
⅛ teaspoon cloves
⅛ teaspoon hot sauce

Dissolve coffee in water. Add orange juice, onion, salt, lemon juice, cloves, and hot sauce. Place steaks in marinade and refrigerate 6 hours or overnight. Place steaks on grill top so surface of meat is 4 to 5 inches from heat, and broil at moderate temperature to rare or medium (25 to 35 minutes), turning and brushing with marinade occasionally.

Courtesy of National Live Stock and Meat Board

Island Steak

6 rib-eye steaks, about 1 inch thick
1 cup soy sauce
1 clove garlic, crushed
¼ cup salad oil
¼ cup dry red wine
Juice from small piece of celery (extracted with
    garlic press)

Combine all ingredients except the steaks. Marinate steaks with this mixture for 30 minutes only. Drain steaks and sear each side for one minute with grill in lowest position over moderate fire. Raise grill to medium position and cook to taste, turning steaks twice. *(6 servings)*

Courtesy of Metals Engineering Corporation

Lemon 'N Spice Beef Steaks

1 or 2 beef blade steaks, cut ½–¾ inch thick
⅔ cup lemon juice
½ cup water
1 tablespoon oil
1 tablespoon sugar
1½ teaspoons salt
1 teaspoon thyme
¼ teaspoon garlic powder

Combine lemon juice, water, oil, sugar, salt, thyme, and garlic powder in small saucepan and cook slowly for 5 minutes. Cool. Place steaks in dish and pour marinade over them, turning to coat. Cover dish and refrigerate 6 hours or overnight, turning at least once. Remove steaks from marinade and place on grill so surface of meat is 4 inches from heat. Broil at moderate temperature 7 to 10 minutes on each side, depending upon degree of doneness desired. Brush occasionally with marinade while broiling.

Courtesy of National Live Stock and Meat Board

Oriental Sesame Steak

½ cup soy sauce
1 tablespoon sesame seeds
¼ cup sake or dry white wine
1 onion, chopped
½ cup chopped green onion
1 clove garlic, crushed
½ teaspoon ginger
3 pounds lean beef steak

Blend seasonings and pour over steak. Marinate overnight. Just before cooking, remove steak from marinade and brush with oil. Cook at medium setting to desired doneness, basting with marinade several times during cooking. Any remaining marinade may be heated and spooned over steaks at the table. *(4–6 servings)*

Courtesy of Charmglow Products

Pepper Grill Steaks

6 beef eye-round steaks, 1 inch thick
Seasoned meat tenderizer
Black pepper

Lightly moisten both sides of steaks with water; sprinkle generously with meat tenderizer. Pierce entire surface of steaks with fork; let stand at room temperature for 15 minutes. Sprinkle both sides of steaks with pepper; press into steaks. Place on grill 4 to 5 inches from coals; cook to desired doneness.

Courtesy of Kikkoman International Inc.

Special Barbecued Flank Steak

2 tablespoons butter
1 clove garlic, crushed
1 can (8 ounces) tomato sauce
½ cup Worcestershire sauce
2 tablespoons lemon juice
½ teaspoon salt
1½ pounds flank steak

Melt butter in a medium saucepan. Add garlic; sauté for one minute. Blend in tomato sauce, Worcestershire sauce, lemon juice, and salt. Bring to boiling point. Reduce heat; simmer uncovered for 5 minutes. Remove from heat and cool thoroughly. Place steak in a shallow pan or baking dish. Pour half of the sauce over steak. Turn so both sides of the steak are covered. Cover and refrigerate for 24 hours. Grill over hot charcoal or broil under a preheated hot broiler for 4 to 5 minutes on each side or until steak is done as desired, brushing occasionally with sauce. Using a sharp knife, cut steak diagonally into thin slices. *(2–3 servings)*

Courtesy of Lea & Perrins

Steak and Vegetables en Brochette

½ cup bottled chili sauce
3 tablespoons red currant jelly
2½ tablespoons Worcestershire sauce
1–1½ pounds flank steak
1 green pepper, cut into 1½-inch chunks
12 cherry tomatoes

Combine chili sauce, currant jelly, and Worcestershire sauce; set aside. Place flank steak in the freezer for 30 minutes; thinly slice on the diagonal. Parboil green pepper for 3 minutes; remove from water.

On 6 long skewers loosely weave steak slices around green pepper chunks and cherry tomatoes. Brush all sides with Worcestershire sauce mixture. Place on a rack over hot charcoal or broil under a preheated hot broiler until beef is cooked as desired, about 6 to 8 minutes, turning occasionally. *(4–6 servings)*

Courtesy of Lea & Perrins

Polynesian Pot Roast

3½–4½-pound pot roast
½ cup soy sauce
½ cup sherry
1 cup water
2 cloves garlic, crushed
1 teaspoon ground ginger
1 teaspoon seasoned pepper

Put meat in heavy-duty plastic bag or glass baking dish. Combine all remaining ingredients and pour over meat. Tightly close bag and turn to coat meat with marinade, or turn meat in baking dish several times to cover with marinade; cover dish. Refrigerate several hours or overnight, turning once or twice.

To cook, lift roast from marinade and place on grill. Reserve marinade. Smoke-cook about 4 or 5 hours, until tender. (6–8 servings)

Courtesy of The Brinkmann Corporation

Smoked Beef Brisket

5–6-pound beef brisket
Red pepper
Garlic salt
Paprika

Trim excess fat off brisket. Pound meat strongly on either side with fist. On each side sprinkle lightly with red pepper, fairly heavily with garlic salt, then cover with paprika. Meat will taste even better if seasoned the night before, or early in the day it is cooked. Smoke 6 to 8 hours. Slice on the diagonal. *(10–12 servings)*

Courtesy of Bosman Industries, Inc.

Butterfly Leg of Lamb

1 package French dressing mix
3½–4-pound boned, split leg of lamb, trimmed of
  fat

Prepare dressing mix according to directions. Place lamb in shallow pan, pour dressing over it, and let stand at least one hour. Remove from marinade and sprinkle generously with seasoned salt. Grill over medium setting 45 to 60 minutes, turning every 10 or 15 minutes and brushing occasionally with marinade. To serve, cut ¼-inch thick slices across the grain. *(8 servings)*

Courtesy of Turco Manufacturing Company

Jelly-Glazed Lamb Shoulder

3–4 pounds lamb shoulder, boned and rolled
1 clove garlic, sliced
1 teaspoon salt
⅛ teaspoon pepper
1½ cups currant or grape jelly
2 tablespoons prepared mustard

Make several slits in lamb and insert garlic slices. Rub meat with salt and pepper. Combine jelly and mustard. Secure lamb on spit and cook at low setting for 1 to 1¾ hours, with lid closed. Open lid and brush meat with jelly-mustard mixture. Set heat at medium and cook about 10 minutes longer, or until baste forms a glaze. *(4–6 servings)*

Courtesy of Charmglow Products

Leg of Lamb Oriental

3½-pound shank half leg of lamb
¼ cup soy sauce
2 tablespoons oil
2 tablespoons honey
½ teaspoon ginger
2 tablespoons dry white wine
½ teaspoon mint leaves
½ teaspoon rosemary leaves, crushed

Insert rotisserie rod lengthwise through leg of lamb, parallel to the bone. Secure with spit forks. Combine remaining 7 ingredients and mix well. Cook lamb on rotisserie 1 inch from heat, allowing about 1½ hours for rare, 2 hours for medium. Brush frequently with sauce. *(4–6 servings)*

Courtesy of Kikkoman International Inc.

Smoked Beef Symphony

3 tablespoons butter
1 pint sour cream
1-pound jar artichoke hearts
½ pound smoked beef, chopped
½ cup dry white wine
2 tablespoons Parmesan cheese

Melt 2 tablespoons of the butter in a double boiler over low heat. Add the sour cream, stirring thoroughly. Separately heat well drained and thinly sliced artichoke hearts with the rest of the butter and the smoked beef.

Add wine and cheese to sour cream. Blend well and add meat-artichoke mixture. Serve on toast or muffins and top with additional grated cheese.

Courtesy of Gladys Jackson/McArthur's Smokehouse

Japanese Smorgasbord

Arrange shrimp, boneless chicken parts, ham, thick zucchini slices, mushrooms, chicken livers, pineapple slices, peach and apricot halves, orange sections, apple rings, chunks of tender beef, and small frankfurters in fingerbowls around the smoker. Make a bowl of equal parts of soy sauce, sherry, and oil to serve as a quick marinade, and let your guests skewer, dip, and cook their own feast.

Courtesy of Charcoal Briquet Institute

Extraordinary Barbecued Short Ribs

4 pounds beef short ribs
¼ cup water
⅓ cup catsup
⅓ cup oil
¼ cup brown sugar
¼ cup vinegar
1½ teaspoons chili powder
1½ teaspoons salt
1 teaspoon onion powder

Put short ribs in heavy plastic bag or deep bowl. Combine all remaining ingredients and pour over ribs. Close bag tightly and turn to coat ribs completely; or spoon marinade over ribs in a glass bowl. Refrigerate several hours or overnight.

To cook, lift ribs from marinade and arrange

on grill. Reserve marinade. Smoke-cook for 4 or 5 hours, until tender. Heat reserved marinade to boiling and serve as sauce. *(4–6 servings)*

Courtesy of The Brinkmann Corporation

Smoky Mountain Spareribs

½ cup Worcestershire sauce
½ cup vinegar
½ teaspoon salt
½ cup butter, melted
¼ teaspoon Tabasco
2 racks spareribs, about 6 pounds

Combine marinade ingredients and brush onto ribs. Use soaked wood chips and indirect cooking. Place meat bone side down on grill. Raise grill to highest position over moderate fire. Lower hood and cook 1½ to 2 hours or until done. Add wood chips and charcoal as necessary to maintain smoke and even heat. Turn and baste ribs every 10 minutes during the last 30 or 40 minutes of cooking time. *(6–8 servings)*

Courtesy of Metals Engineering Corporation

Dilly Grilled Frank Kebabs

1 envelope (1½ ounces) Seasoning Mix for
   Sloppy Joes
¼ cup catsup
¼ cup vinegar
2 tablespoons honey or light corn syrup
1 pound frankfurters, cut in thirds
8–10 dill pickles, cut in half
8–10 slices of bacon
8–10 frankfurter rolls

Combine contents of seasoning mix envelope,
catsup, vinegar, and honey in a small mixing
bowl or jar. Alternate frankfurter and pickle
chunks on 8 to 10 skewers, weaving bacon
around them. Brush with seasoning mixture.
Grill over hot coals or broil, for 8 to 10 minutes,
turning once and brushing with remaining seasoning mixture. Serve on frankfurter rolls.

Courtesy of R. T. French Company

Beef Steak Kebabs

2 pounds beef steak, cut in cubes
2 medium-sized onions, sliced and quartered into
   wedges
1 dozen mushroom caps
2 tomatoes, cut in wedges
2 green peppers, cut in squares

Put beef cubes in marinade of your choice for a minimum of 2 hours. String beef and vegetables alternately on skewers. Paint with remaining marinade and smoke for about 45 minutes. *(4–6 servings)*

Courtesy of Bosman Industries, Inc.

Ham Kebabs

Precooked ham steak, diced
Pineapple chunks
½ cup pineapple juice
½ cup honey or brown sugar

Blend pineapple juice and honey or sugar over low heat. Alternate ham and pineapple on skewers. Paint with sauce and smoke for 45 minutes. Parboiled sweet potato chunks can also be added.

Courtesy of Bosman Industries, Inc.

Lamb Kebabs

1½ pounds boned shoulder of lamb
Salt and pepper to taste
Dash powdered ginger
¼ cup soy sauce
2 tablespoons vinegar
½ cup salad oil
4 slices bacon, cut in 1-inch squares
1 cup pineapple chunks

Cut meat into 1-inch cubes. Season with salt and pepper and ginger. Combine soy sauce with vinegar and oil and pour over the meat. Marinate 30 minutes or longer. Arrange lamb on skewers alternately with bacon and chunks of pineapple. Broil 3 inches from heat for about 15 minutes, turning once or twice to brown evenly. Baste with marinade while cooking. *(4–6 servings)*

Courtesy of Kikkoman International Inc.

Party Kebabs

4 pounds sirloin or top round steak, ¾–1 inch
  thick
3 ounces bleu cheese
2 tablespoons sour cream
16–20 prunes, pitted
6–7 pieces of bacon, cut into thirds
16–20 mushrooms
½ cup beer
½ cup cooking oil

Mix bleu cheese and sour cream together. Stuff
each prune with mixture and wrap with a piece
of bacon, securing with a wooden toothpick.
Skewer beef chunks, mushrooms, and prunes alternately. Place in shallow glass baking dish. Mix
together beer and oil. Pour over kebabs. Let
marinate at least one hour before cooking, turning occasionally. Place on greased grill and
smoke at medium setting for about 10 minutes,
turning frequently, or until meat is browned and
cooked to desired doneness. *(8–10 servings)*

Courtesy of Charmglow Products

Spicy Ribs and Fruit Kebabs

4–6 pounds pork back ribs
1 jar (16 ounces) spiced crab apples
1 jar (10 ounces) sweet pickled watermelon rind
2 teaspoons cornstarch
Salt and pepper

Drain crab apples and pickled watermelon; reserve syrups and gradually add to cornstarch, stirring to blend. Cook, stirring constantly until thickened. Reduce heat and cook slowly for one minute. Place ribs on grill top so surface of meat is approximately 5 inches (or more) from heat. Broil at low to moderate temperature for 45 minutes to one hour, turning occasionally. Thread crab apples and watermelon rind alternately on metal skewers and place over heat. Season ribs with salt and pepper and brush with syrup. Broil ribs and kebabs 10 to 15 minutes or until meat is done, turning and brushing occasionally. *(4–6 servings)*

Courtesy of National Livestock and Meat Board

Western Kebabs

2 pounds boneless tender beef steak
½ cup teriyaki sauce
2 tablespoons salad oil
1 cup pineapple chunks, drained, or fresh pineapple, chunked
1 pint cherry tomatoes

Cut meat into 1-inch cubes; pierce meat with fork so marinade can penetrate. Combine teriyaki sauce and oil; pour over meat cubes and marinate one hour, turning occasionally. Thread meat on skewers, leaving space between pieces. Thread pineapple and tomatoes together on separate skewers. Place on grill 4 to 5 inches from heat and cook for 15 minutes. Turn meat over and place remaining skewers on grill. Brush food with marinade and cook to desired doneness. *(4–6 servings)*

Courtesy of Kikkoman International Inc.

Frankburgers

Roll lean ground beef into shape and size of a hot dog. Wrap with bacon and pin ends with wooden toothpicks. Cook over moderate fire and turn frequently until bacon is crisp. Serve on hot dog bun with relish, mustard, or catsup.

Courtesy of Metals Engineering Corporation

Whirling Franks on a Spit

1 pound frankfurters
10 whole sweet or dill pickles
½ cup barbecue sauce
2 tablespoons prepared mustard
1 teaspoon horseradish
Warm frankfurter buns

Make cross-cut in center of franks and pickles. Insert spit rod through cuts, alternate franks and pickles. Cook on rotisserie for 20 minutes, brushing frequently with sauce.

Courtesy of Metals Engineering Corporation

Hasty-Tasty Hamburgers

2 pounds ground beef
¼ cup soy sauce
2 tablespoons minced onion
1 teaspoon lemon and pepper seasoning
½ teaspoon dry mustard

Thoroughly combine all ingredients; let stand for 10 minutes. Shape into 6 or 8 patties. Cook on grill 3 inches from heat to desired degree of doneness. *(4–6 servings)*

Courtesy of Kikkoman International Inc.

Juicy Burgers

1 beef bouillon cube
½ cup boiling water
1 pound ground beef
⅓ cup dry bread crumbs
1 teaspoon grated lemon peel
Juice of 1 lemon
½ teaspoon salt
½ teaspoon pepper
½ teaspoon ground sage
½ teaspoon ginger
4–5 hamburger buns, toasted

Dissolve bouillon cube in boiling water. Mix thoroughly with beef, crumbs, lemon peel and lemon juice, and seasonings. Shape into 4 or 5 patties and chill thoroughly. Grill in highest position until done, about 7 minutes per side. Serve on toasted buns. *(2–4 servings)*

Courtesy of Metals Engineering Corporation

Teriyaki Surprise Burgers

1½ pounds ground beef
¼ cup soft bread crumbs
2 tablespoons minced onion
½ teaspoon garlic powder
6 tablespoons teriyaki sauce
6 pineapple slices, drained

Combine first 4 ingredients with 4 tablespoons teriyaki sauce; mix well. Shape mixture into 12 thin patties. Place one slice of pineapple on each of 6 patties. Top with remaining patties; pinch edges together to seal. Cook on grill 3 to 5 inches from coals, for about 5 minutes or to desired doneness. Brush burgers frequently with remaining teriyaki sauce as they cook. *(2–3 servings)*

Courtesy of Kikkoman International Inc.

Hams aging in a Virginia smokehouse. *ITT Gwaltney Inc.*

Larger smoke cookers provide room to prepare several kinds of food at the same time. *W. C. Bradley Co.*

Chicken and corn can be cooked simultaneously on the Smoke 'N Pit Charcoal-Water Smoker. *The Brinkmann Corporation*

Smoked turkey atop Cook'N Ca'Jun Charcoal-Water Smoker.
Bosman Industries Inc.

Two sizes of Smoke 'N Pit Electric Smokers. Note accessory shelves on the model in the background. *The Brinkmann Corporation*

This gas-powered smoker has a lid and a control knob which regulates the cooking flame. *Turco Manufacturing Company*

Model of metal cooking grill with hood. *Metals Engineering Corporation*

Metal smoker grill with detachable wing table and leg shelf. *Metals Engineering Corporation*

Metal smoker grill showing attached rotisserie unit. *Metals Engineering Corporation*

Wineburgers

2 pounds ground beef chuck
2 teaspoons Worcestershire sauce
2 tablespoons minced onion
2 teaspoons prepared mustard
⅓ cup catsup
2 teaspoons horseradish
½ cup fine, dry bread crumbs
½ cup dry red wine
1 clove garlic, crushed
1 teaspoon salt
¼ teaspoon pepper

Combine ingredients and shape into 8 patties, about 1 inch thick. Brush with melted butter. Place on hot grill and brown slowly on both sides until done, 10 to 20 minutes. *(4–6 servings)*

Courtesy of W. C. Bradley Co.

POULTRY

GUIDE TO SMOKE COOKING POULTRY ON A GRILL

Food	Setting for Electric Smokers	Setting for Gas Smokers	Approx. Cooking Time	Special Instructions
CHICKEN Whole (broiler-fryer) 2 to 3 lb.	4	Low or Medium Flame	1 hr. to 1 hr. 30 min.	Season. Grill, turning and brushing frequently with melted butter, margarine, salad oil, or marinade.
Halved or Quartered	4	Low or Medium Flame	40 to 60 min.	Season. Place skin side away from burner, on grid. Grill, turning and brushing frequently with melted butter, margarine, salad oil, or marinade.
TURKEY Whole (ready-to-eat) 10 to 14 lb.	4	Low Flame	Approx. 20 min. per pound. Add 5 min. per pound if stuffed	Place in shallow pan on grid. Cook with hood down. Bird is done when thermometer registers 185°F. if inserted in thigh; 165°F. if inserted in stuffing.
Pieces, Halves, Quarters 5 to 6 lb.	4	Low Flame	45 min. to 1 hr.	Same as above.

GUIDE TO COOKING POULTRY ON THE ROTISSERIE

Food	Setting for Electric Smokers	Setting for Gas Smokers	Approx. Cooking Time	Special Instructions
CHICKEN Whole (broiler-fryer) 2 to 3 lb.	4	Low to Medium Flame	1 hr. 30 min. to 2 hr. 30 min.	Season cavity. Tie legs to tail and wings to body. Brush skin with melted butter, margarine, or salad oil. Season. Insert spit through center of bird. Fasten with holding forks. Check for balance by cradling spit in hands and rotating. Reposition spit if necessary. When cooking more than one bird, place on spit in same direction, pushing close together. Fasten cord to spit and tie birds, criss-cross fashion. Fasten with holding forks.

DUCK (domestic) 3 to 5 lb.	4	Low to Medium Flame	2 hr. to 3 hr. 30 min.	Season cavity. Tie legs to tail and wings to body. Sprinkle with paprika. Note: Domestic duck contains much fat so do not brush with butter or margarine.
CORNISH HEN 1 lb.	4	Medium to High Flame	1 hr. to 1 hr. 30 min.	Season cavity. Tie legs to tail and wings to body. Brush skin with melted butter, margarine, or salad oil. Season. See Chicken.
TURKEY Boneless Roll (frozen) 3 to 5 lb. (175°)	5	Low Flame	2 hr. to 2 hr. 30 min.	Thaw. Brush skin with melted butter, margarine, or salad oil. Season.
Whole—6 to 8 lb.	5	Low to Medium Flame	3 hr. to 4 hr. 30 min.	Season cavity. Tie legs to tail and wings to body. Brush skin with melted butter, margarine, or salad oil. Season.

120

Courtesy of Turco Manufacturing Company

COOKING CHART

CHARCOAL-WATER SMOKERS

Poultry	Weight*	Charcoal	Wood	Water	Cooking Time
Turkey	8-12 lbs.	10 lbs.	3 sticks	6 qt.	8-10 hrs.
	13-16 lbs.	12 lbs.	3 sticks	7 qt.	10-12 hrs.
	17-20 lbs.	15 lbs.	3 sticks	8 qt.	12-14 hrs.
Fryers	2½ lb. avg. 1 to 4 chickens	6 lbs.	2 sticks	5 qt.	4-5 hrs.
Hens	5 lb. avg. 1-3 hens	8 lbs.	3 sticks	6 qt.	6-7 hrs.

General Rule: Hardwood briquettes will burn approximately 1 hour per lb.

Meats not listed will cook at the rate of approximately 1 hour per pound (minimum 5 lbs. hardwood briquettes)

Cooking time is determined by the largest single piece being cooked.

Additional charcoal is not required for cooking on 2 or more levels.

*Weights given for each grill level.

Courtesy of Bosman Industries

Duck à l'Orange

4–5-pound duckling
1 cup orange juice
1 tablespoon grated orange peel
1 cup sauterne or other white wine
1 teaspoon garlic, onion, or celery salt
1 onion, quartered
1 apple, quartered
3 stalks celery, including leaves, sliced

Put duckling in deep bowl. Combine orange juice and peel, wine and salt, and pour over duck. Marinate overnight in refrigerator. Lift duckling from marinade. Put onion, apple, and celery in cavity; put on grill. Smoke-cook about 6 to 8 hours or until leg can be moved easily in joint. (With smokers that have water pans, pour marinade in from start of cooking for maximum flavor.) *(4–5 servings)*

Courtesy of The Brinkmann Corporation

Champion Chicken

5-pound roasting chicken, or 2–3 whole fryers, or 2–3 split or cut-up fryers
2 cups beer, white wine, Italian or garlic salad dressing, lemonade or limeade, ginger ale, or any other marinade of your choice

Put chicken in heavy-duty plastic bag or deep
bowl and pour marinade over. Close bag or
cover bowl and refrigerate for several hours or
overnight, turning chicken in marinade occasionally. Lift chicken from marinade and put on
cooking grill or in rib rack on grill. (Add marinade to water pan, if using a smoker that is so
equipped.) Smoke about 4 to 5 hours for halved
or cut-up chickens, 5 hours for whole fryers, and
6 to 7 hours for roasting chicken. When done,
leg will move easily in joint. Use remaining
juices to make sauce or gravy. *(4–6 servings)*

Courtesy of Smoke 'N Pit Corporation

Chicken Dandy

2 chickens, cut in quarters
¼ cup Worcestershire sauce
¼ cup oil
¼ cup vinegar
1 teaspoon celery salt
½ teaspoon onion powder
**¼ teaspoon each of basil, marjoram, and rose-
mary**

Combine all ingredients. Pour over uncooked,
quartered chickens. Refrigerate for one hour.
Drain and save liquid. Brush on chicken as it
cooks. Serve chicken with sauce made by combining ⅓ cup reserved liquid, 1 can (6 ounces)
tomato paste, and 2 tablespoons sugar. Bring

123

ingredients to boil, simmer for 10 minutes, and pour over cooked chickens. *(3–6 servings)*

Courtesy of R. T. French Company

Chili Chicken Barbecue

1 can (10 ounces) tomatoes and green chilies
1 tablespoon minced onion
2 tablespoons oil
2 teaspoons chili powder
1½ teaspoons Season-All
2½-pound chicken, quartered

In blender jar combine first 5 ingredients. Blend for one minute at low speed. Rinse and dry chicken; place on grill 5 to 6 inches from heat. Cook 1½ hours, turning every 15 minutes. Brush frequently with sauce. *(3–6 servings)*

Courtesy of Kikkoman International Inc.

Grilled Tarragon Chicken

½ cup melted butter
¾–1 teaspoon dried tarragon
1 clove garlic, crushed
6 broiler-fryer halves (1–1¼ pounds each)

Combine butter, tarragon, and garlic in saucepan and simmer over low heat for 3 minutes. Brush chicken with sauce and place bone side down on grill. Cook over medium setting for 20 minutes. Turn and continue grilling for 20 to 30 minutes, brushing with sauce several times. (6–8 servings)

Courtesy of Turco Manufacturing Company

Lemon Ginger Chicken

Select a large, plump chicken, 4 to 6 pounds. Combine 1 can frozen, undiluted lemonade, dash ground ginger, and salt and pepper to taste in a dish. Spoon over chicken. Cook 30 minutes on each side, or until done. (4–6 servings)

Courtesy of Charcoal Briquet Institute

Lemon-Up Chicken

2½–3-pound broiler-fryer, cut up
½ cup oil
¼ cup lemon juice
¼ cup water
2 teaspoons garlic salt
1 teaspoon Italian seasoning
½ teaspoon black pepper

Rinse and dry chicken. Combine remaining ingredients; pour over chicken. Cover and marinate in refrigerator for 2 hours. Remove chicken from marinade; place on grill 6 to 8 inches from heat. Cook 20 to 25 minutes on each side. Baste with marinade during last 15 minutes of cooking time.

Courtesy of Kikkoman International Inc.

Luau Chicken

Combine ½ cup teriyaki sauce, ½ teaspoon each ginger, lemon-and-pepper seasoning. Place 3-pound cut-up broiler-fryer chicken in large plastic bag; add sauce, press air out, and close bag securely. Refrigerate for 5 to 6 hours or overnight, turning occasionally. Remove chicken; reserve marinade. Place on grill 5 to 6 inches from coals. Cook for 20 minutes on each side or until done; baste with marinade during last 15 minutes of cooking. *(3–4 servings)*

Courtesy of Kikkoman International Inc.

Mexican Chicken

1 8-ounce can tomato sauce
1 tablespoon parsley flakes
1 tablespoon sugar
1 teaspoon salt
½ teaspoon chili sauce
⅛ teaspoon pepper
⅛ teaspoon Tabasco sauce
2 broiler-fryer chickens (2 pounds each), split in halves

Combine tomato sauce and seasonings. Place chicken halves, bone side down, on grill. Adjust to medium position over moderate coals and cook 20 to 30 minutes. Turn chicken and cook 30 to 40 minutes more. Turn chicken frequently and brush on tomato mixture. *(4–6 servings)*

Courtesy of Metals Engineering Corporation

Quick Oriental Chicken

Brush pieces of chicken with duck sauce or preserves: pineapple, cherry, peach, or orange marmalade. Wrap chicken in heavy-duty aluminum foil with one package of frozen vegetables or an equal amount of leftover vegetables. Poke a few holes in the top and smoke on grill until done.

Courtesy of Charcoal Briquet Institute

Apple Flavored Turkey

1 turkey
½ cup salt
½ cup sugar
1 quart apple or cranberry juice
1 teaspoon rosemary
1 teaspoon sweet basil
Honey for basting

Combine all ingredients except honey and marinate turkey in the mixture for 8 to 12 hours. Remove bird, rinse, and air dry. Preheat smoker and place turkey on the rack. Open upper and lower cavities to expose insides to smoke flavor. Smoke with apple chips or fuel allowing 30 minutes per pound.

Remove from smoker and bake in oven at 300°F., allowing 15 minutes per pound. Baste with honey during the last hour of cooking.

Courtesy of Luhr Jensen and Sons, Inc.

Parmesan Turkeyburgers

1 pound raw turkey
2 tablespoons grated Parmesan cheese
2 tablespoons dry bread crumbs
2 tablespoons tomato catsup
1 teaspoon Season-All
½ teaspoon oregano
½ teaspoon salt
½ teaspoon paprika

Combine all ingredients; mix lightly. Shape into 4 patties. Cook on grill 3 to 4 inches from moderate coals for 10 to 15 minutes or until well done. *(4 servings)*

Courtesy of Kikkoman International Inc.

Southern-Style Smoked Chicken

2 3-pound chickens, whole or halved
1 bottle (20 ounces) barbecue sauce
1 can warm beer
2 lemons, cut in slices
½ cup chopped onions

Select the fuel of your choice, light it, and when temperature can be regulated to low, place birds on grill. Smoke 15 minutes per pound, with hood closed. While they are smoking, mix barbecue sauce with one can of beer. After one hour of smoking, place lemon slices on chicken, sprinkle onions on top. Pour sauce over chicken. Cover and cook for another 30 minutes. *(6–8 servings)*

Courtesy of Charmglow Products

Smoked Game Hens

Spear whole game hens, end to end. Wrap in bacon and stuff with wedges of unpeeled orange. Brush with Italian salad dressing and use a drip pan in the front of the grill to catch the drippings. Cook until legs and wings move, and meat can be pierced easily. (Small whole chickens can be cooked the same way.)

Courtesy of Charcoal Briquet Institute

SEAFOOD

GUIDE TO SMOKE COOKING SEAFOOD ON A GRILL

Food	Setting for Electric Smokers	Setting for Gas Smokers	Approx. Cooking Time	Special Instructions
Breaded, Precooked Fish (frozen) Fillets, Sticks	High	Medium to High Flame	8 to 12 min.	Grill, turning once.
Fish Steaks ¾ to 1 inch thick	5	Medium to High Flame	8 to 15 min.	Season. If desired, sprinkle with paprika for additional color. Grill, turning once and brushing occasionally with melted butter, margarine, or salad oil to keep moist.
Whole Fish 4 to 8 oz.	5	Medium to High Flame	12 to 20 min.	Season. If desired, sprinkle with paprika for additional color. Grill, turning once and brushing occasionally with melted butter, margarine, or salad oil to keep moist.

Lobster Tails—3 to 5 oz.	5	Medium to High Flame	10 to 15 min.	Remove and discard undershell. Season. If desired, sprinkle with paprika for additional color. Insert skewer lengthwise through tail or clamp tightly in double wire broiler to prevent curling. Grill, turning once and brushing occasionally with melted butter, margarine, or salad oil to keep moist.
Lobster Whole—1½ lb. Halved	5	Medium to High Flame	15 to 20 min.	Crack claws. Season. Place shell side toward burner, on grid. Grill, turning once and brushing occasionally with melted butter, margarine, or salad oil to keep moist.

133

Courtesy of Turco Manufacturing Company

COOKING CHART

CHARCOAL-WATER SMOKERS

Seafood	Weight*	Charcoal	Wood	Water	Cooking Time
Fish	grill full	5 lbs.	2 sticks	5 qt.	1½-2½ hrs.
Shrimp	jumbo	5 lbs.	1 stick	4 qt.	1½-2½ hrs.

General Rule: Hardwood briquettes will burn approximately 1 hour per lb.

Meats not listed will cook at the rate of approximately 1 hour per pound (minimum 5 lbs. hardwood briquettes)

Cooking time is determined by the largest single piece being cooked.

Additional charcoal is not required for cooking on 2 or more levels.

*Weights given for each grill level.

Courtesy of Bosman Industries

Hickory Smoked Sablefish

2 pounds sablefish steaks, or any other fish steaks, fresh or frozen
⅓ cup soy sauce
2 tablespoons melted fat or oil
1 tablespoon Liquid Smoke
1 clove garlic, finely chopped
½ teaspoon ginger

Thaw frozen steaks. Cut into serving-size portions and place in a single layer in a shallow baking dish. Combine remaining ingredients. Pour over fish and let stand for 30 minutes, turning once. Remove fish, reserving sauce for basting. Place fish on grill and cook about 4 inches from moderately hot coals for 8 minutes. Baste with sauce. Turn and cook 7 to 10 minutes longer until fish flakes easily when tested with a fork. (6 servings)

Courtesy of National Marine Fisheries Service

Italian Style Salmon Steaks

2 pounds salmon steaks or other fish steaks, fresh
  or frozen
2 cups Italian dressing
2 tablespoons lemon juice
2 teaspoons salt
¼ teaspoon pepper
Paprika

Thaw frozen steaks. Cut into serving-size portions and place in a single layer in a shallow baking dish. Combine remaining ingredients except
paprika. Pour sauce over fish and let stand for
30 minutes, turning once. Remove fish, reserving
sauce for basting. Sprinkle with paprika. Place
fish on grill and cook about 4 inches from moderately hot smoking coals for 8 minutes. Baste
with sauce and sprinkle again with paprika. Turn
and cook for 7 to 10 minutes longer or until fish
flakes easily when tested with a fork. *(6 servings)*

Courtesy of National Marine Fisheries Service

Salmon Steaks Caribbean

6 salmon steaks, 1 inch thick
⅓ cup dry white wine
⅓ cup lime juice
¼ teaspoon white pepper
1¼ teaspoons onion salt
¾ cup dairy sour cream
1 tablespoon chopped chives
1 teaspoon butter

Rinse and dry salmon steaks; arrange in single layer in dish just large enough to hold steaks. Combine next 3 ingredients and 1 teaspoon of onion salt; pour over salmon. Cover and refrigerate for 1 to 2 hours; baste occasionally. Remove from marinade; place on grill 4 inches from coals. Cook 5 minutes on each side. Brush often with marinade while cooking. Combine ¼ cup marinade with remaining onion salt, sour cream, chives, and butter. Heat, stirring, until butter melts and sauce is hot. Do not boil. Serve salmon with sauce. (6 servings)

Courtesy of Kikkoman International Inc.

Oriental Swordfish Steaks

2 **pounds swordfish steaks or other fish fillets, fresh or frozen**
¼ **cup orange juice**
¼ **cup soy sauce**
2 **tablespoons catsup**
2 **tablespoons melted fat or oil**
2 **tablespoons chopped parsley**
1 **tablespoon lemon juice**
1 **clove garlic**
½ **teaspoon oregano**
½ **teaspoon pepper**

Thaw frozen steaks. Cut into serving-size portions and place in a single layer in a shallow baking dish. Combine remaining ingredients. Pour sauce over fish and let stand for 30 minutes, turning once. Remove fish, reserving sauce for basting. Place fish on grill and cook about 4 inches from moderately hot smoking coals for 8 minutes. Baste with sauce. Turn and cook for 7 to 10 minutes longer or until fish flakes easily when tested with a fork. *(6 servings)*

Courtesy of National Marine Fisheries Service

Savory Soft-Shell Crabs

12 dressed soft-shell crabs, fresh or frozen
¾ cup chopped parsley
¼ cup fat or oil
1 teaspoon lemon juice
¼ teaspoon nutmeg
¼ teaspoon soy sauce
Dash liquid hot pepper sauce
Lemon wedges

Thaw frozen crabs. Clean, wash, and dry crabs. Place crabs in well-greased, hinged wire grill or smoker. Combine remaining ingredients except lemon. Heat. Baste crabs with sauce. Cook about 4 inches from moderately hot coals for 8 minutes. Baste with sauce. Turn and cook 7 to 10 minutes or until lightly browned. Serve with lemon. *(6 servings)*

Courtesy of National Marine Fisheries Service

Smoked Fish

1 quart water
¼ cup salt
2–3 pounds fresh or frozen thawed fish fillets, steaks, or small whole dressed fish
1 tablespoon dried tarragon leaves (optional)

Mix water and salt until salt dissolves. Pour into large glass baking dish or other shallow container. Arrange fish fillets, steaks, or whole butterflied fish in brine, cover, and refrigerate several hours or overnight. Before starting fire or preparing smoker, lift fish from brine and arrange on wire racks to air dry for 20 to 30 minutes. Be sure to grease grill. Arrange fish in single layer on grill, leaving space between pieces if possible. (Add tarragon to water pan if this type of smoker is used.) Smoke-cook 2 to 3 hours over charcoal (1 to 2½ hours for electric) or until fish flakes with a fork. *(4–6 servings)*

Courtesy of The Brinkmann Corporation

Smoked Fish Fillets

3 pounds fish fillets
1 stick butter, melted
Juice of 1 lemon
½ teaspoon Worcestershire sauce
5–6 dashes Tabasco sauce
¼ cup chopped parsley

Make a tray with 2-inch sides from heavy aluminum foil. Place fillets in a single layer. Combine butter, lemon juice, sauces, and parsley, and pour over fish. Place on grill in smoker, cover with top, and cook for 1 to 2 hours. *(6 servings)*

Courtesy of Bosman Industries, Inc.

Smoked Trout

4 brook trout
2 strips bacon
1 cup butter
1 teaspoon garlic salt
Salt and pepper to taste
1 lemon cut in wedges

Clean fish. Construct small aluminum boat for each fish. Place ½ strip of bacon on top of fish and place in boat. Light grill and set temperature on medium heat. Cook for 15 minutes with hood closed, or until bacon is done.

Turn heat to low. Pour mixed melted butter and garlic salt on fish. Let simmer for 3 minutes. Add salt and pepper to taste. Serve hot with lemon wedges. *(4 servings)*

Courtesy of Charmglow Products

Rainbow Trout and Bacon

6 rainbow trout, fresh or frozen, cleaned
2 tablespoons condensed milk
½ teaspoon garlic salt
2 tablespoons minced parsley
½ teaspoon nutmeg or allspice
12 slices bacon
Lemon wedges

Blend milk, garlic salt, parsley, and nutmeg. Coat trout inside and out with mixture. Wrap bacon around trout and secure with pick. Place on oiled, preheated grill and cook at medium setting for 15 to 20 minutes, turning so bacon cooks evenly. Serve with additional parsley and lemon wedges. *(6 servings)*

Courtesy of Charmglow Products

Smoked Lobster or Shrimp

2–3 pounds peeled deveined shrimp, thawed or fresh, or 4–6 8-ounce lobster tails, butterflied
Melted butter
Lemon juice

Brush shrimp or lobster with mixture of melted butter and lemon juice. Put small shrimp on tray made from aluminum foil; larger shrimp and lobster tails can go in a single layer right on a well-greased grill. Smoke-cook about 1 to 2 hours (depending on size) until firm. *(4–6 servings)*

Courtesy of The Brinkmann Corporation

Shrimp Kebabs

1½ pounds fresh shrimp, or frozen shrimp, thawed
3 tablespoons butter, melted
1 tablespoon lemon juice
½ teaspoon salt
⅛ teaspoon pepper
4 slices bacon, cut in squares
1 4-ounce can button mushrooms, drained

Combine butter, lemon juice, and salt and pepper. Peel, devein, and wash shrimp, and pat dry with paper towels. Alternate shrimp, bacon squares, and mushrooms on skewers and brush with the seasoned butter. Place on preheated grill. Cook at medium setting for about 5 minutes. Turn and brush with more butter and broil for 3 to 5 minutes longer. Serve with lemon wedges.

Courtesy of Charmglow Products

Smoked Mullet

6 dressed mullet (1 pound each) or other dressed fish, fresh or frozen
1 cup salt
1 gallon water
¼ cup salad oil

Thaw frozen fish. Remove the head and cut along the backbone almost to the tail. The fish should lie flat in one piece. Clean and wash fish. Add salt to water and stir until dissolved. Add fish to brine and let stand for 30 minutes. Remove fish from brine and rinse in cold water.

To smoke the fish, use a charcoal fire in a barbecue grill with a cover or hood.

Place fish on well-greased grill, skin side down, about 4 inches from the smoking coals. Cover and smoke for 1½ hours. Add remaining chips as needed to keep the fire smoking.

Increase temperature by adding more charcoal and opening the draft. Brush fish with oil. Cover and cook 15 minutes longer. Brush fish again with oil. Cover and cook 10 minutes longer or until fish is lightly browned. *(6 servings)*

Courtesy of National Marine Fisheries Service

Smoked Red Snapper Steaks

2 pounds red snapper steaks, or other fish steaks, fresh or frozen
½ cup melted fat or oil
¼ cup lemon juice
2 teaspoons salt
½ teaspoon Worcestershire sauce
¼ teaspoon white pepper
Dash liquid hot pepper sauce
Paprika

Thaw frozen steaks. Cut into serving-size portions and place in well-greased, hinged wire grills. Combine remaining ingredients except paprika. Baste fish with sauce and sprinkle with paprika. Cook about 4 inches from moderately hot coals for 8 minutes. Baste with sauce and sprinkle with paprika. Turn and cook for 7 to 10 minutes longer, or until fish flakes easily when tested with a fork. *(6 servings)*

Courtesy of National Marine Fisheries Service

Smoked Lobster Tails

Remove and discard undershell. Season. If desired, sprinkle with paprika for additional color. Insert skewer lengthwise through tail or clamp tightly in double wire broiler to prevent curling. Grill over smoking coals, turning once and brushing occasionally with melted butter to keep moist.

Courtesy of W. C. Bradley Co.

Stuffed Crab

1 pound crab meat
⅓ cup butter melted
2 tablespoons lemon juice
¼ teaspoon salt
Dash of cayenne pepper
6 crab shells, washed and greased
¼ cup chopped parsley

Pick over crab meat, removing any shell or cartilage. Combine butter, lemon juice, salt, cayenne, and crab meat. Place in prepared shells, and wrap each crab individually in double thicknesses of heavy-duty foil. Place over coals and cook on low for 12 to 16 minutes or until done. Garnish with chopped parsley. *(4 servings)*

Courtesy of Charmglow Products

VEGETABLES

Lemon Asparagus Tips

Top a package of frozen asparagus tips with butter, salt, pepper, and juice of one fresh lemon. Wrap in heavy-duty aluminum foil and cook over smoking embers.

Courtesy of Charcoal Briquet Institute

Corn and Asparagus au Gratin

2 packages frozen asparagus
1 package frozen corn kernels
20-30 fresh mushrooms
1 can undiluted cream of celery soup
½ cup stuffed green olives, sliced
Salt and pepper to taste
Dash paprika
Bread crumbs
Grated cheese

Combine first 5 ingredients in a casserole. Season to taste with salt, pepper, and paprika. Cover with a thin layer of bread crumbs and sprinkle with grated cheese. Smoke simultaneously with the entree until heated through.

Courtesy Bosman Industries, Inc.

Baked Beans I

Open a can of baked beans or pork and beans and turn into casserole or pouch made from heavy-duty aluminum foil. Cover or not, depending on whether you want the beans smoked or just heated along with a smoke-cooked entree. Put on grill for 1 to 2 hours.

Courtesy of The Brinkmann Corporation

Baked Beans II

4–5 pounds canned pork and beans
½ cup chopped onion
¼ cup chopped celery
⅓ cup chopped bell peppers
2 tablespoons prepared mustard
½ cup molasses or ribbon cane syrup
1 teaspoon Worcestershire sauce
5 shakes Tabasco sauce
½ cup barbecue sauce
½ cup catsup
2 strips bacon, uncooked and cut in halves

Combine all ingredients except bacon in large, ovenproof container. Lay bacon strips on top. Cook on upper tray simultaneously with meat, until bubbling. If desired, browned ground meat can be added to the beans.

Courtesy of Bosman Industries, Inc.

Roast Corn, Italian Style

Turn back husks and strip off silk. Lay husks in position. Soak ears in cold water for 5 minutes. Line ears up on grill over hot coals. Keep turning ears frequently. Cook for 15 to 20 minutes or until husks are dry and browned. (Corn will look suntanned.) Dunking ears in a pail of water occasionally will keep kernels moist. To serve, break off husks and provide plenty of butter.

Courtesy of W. C. Bradley Co.

Baked Potatoes I

Scrub potatoes and rub skins with melted butter or oil. Medium potatoes will bake in 4 to 5 hours; large potatoes will take longer.

Courtesy of The Brinkmann Corporation

Baked Potatoes II

Insert an aluminum baking nail through the center of a baking potato. Let nail extend on each end. Place potatoes around side of grill, leaving room for cooking steaks or roast. Cook 40 to 50 minutes over moderate fire. Garnish by cutting an X at the top of each potato. Push in each of the four corners and add butter and seasoning.

Courtesy of Metals Engineering Corporation

Bacon-Baked Potatoes

Scrub medium baking potatoes and cut in half the long way. Put ½ slice bacon in between each potato slice and fasten with wooden picks. Put on grill with meat and bake for 5 to 6 hours.

Courtesy of The Brinkmann Corporation

Potato-Tomato Accordions

Alternate slices of potatoes with slices of tomatoes. Divide into serving portions, sprinkle with grated cheese, and wrap in foil packets. Place directly on smoking embers (turning occasionally) and cook until potatoes are soft, approximately 30 minutes.

Courtesy of Charcoal Briquet Institute

Herbed Tomato or Onion Slices

Make a tray from heavy-duty aluminum foil that will fit the extra space on your cooking grill. Melt enough butter to just cover the bottom of the tray and pour in. Slice tomatoes ½ inch thick, onions ¼ inch thick, and arrange in single layer on tray. Sprinkle with salt, pepper, basil, fennel, or any other herb. Smoke-cook for 2 to 3 hours.

Courtesy of The Brinkmann Corporation

Green Beans Amandine

2 cans green beans
1 can undiluted cream of mushroom soup
1 can drained mushrooms
2 chopped pimientos
½ cup slivered almonds
Salt and pepper to taste

Mix ingredients together in overproof dish. Great with beef or turkey.

Courtesy of Bosman Industries, Inc.

Green Beans Supreme

2 1-pound cans string beans
1 4-ounce can whole button mushrooms
1 can cream of mushroom soup
⅓ cup milk
2 tablespoons mayonnaise
1 teaspoon soy sauce
1 ounce dry white vermouth
½ teaspoon garlic salt
Pinch of red pepper
Seasoned pepper
¼ cup slivered almonds
⅓ cup toasted bread crumbs
Paprika

Drain and rinse beans thoroughly. Mix with mushrooms and place on bottom of a 2-quart ovenproof casserole. Combine soup, milk, mayonnaise, soy sauce, vermouth, garlic salt, red pepper, and seasoned pepper in bowl and mix well. Spoon mixture over top of beans. Sprinkle with almonds, then bread crumbs, then paprika. Cover with a tight lid or foil and bake on a smoking grill for 2 hours or longer.

Courtesy of Bosman Industries, Inc.

Skewered Western Vegetables

Marinate any or all of the following in bottled Italian-style dressing for ½ hour before cooking: green pepper strips; whole mushrooms; cherry tomatoes; cubes of eggplant; cubes of zucchini or yellow crook-neck squash. Thread vegetables alternately on skewers. Grill until tender and lightly browned, 5 to 8 minutes, brushing occasionally with dressing.

Courtesy of Kikkoman International, Inc.

Stuffed Tomatoes

6 whole tomatoes
6 hard-boiled eggs, chopped
10 tablespoons chopped smoked beef
9 tablespoons mayonnaise
9 tablespoons chopped celery
3 teaspoons chopped green pepper
3 teaspoons prepared mustard
1 teaspoon chopped parsley

Core each tomato and cut ¾ of the way through with a sharp knife. Then cut in half. Combine remaining ingredients and stuff tomatoes with the mixture. Garnish with black olives, additional parsley, and paprika.

This is a great idea for using up tomatoes at harvest time.

Courtesy of McArthur's Smokehouse

Vegetable Casseroles

To simultaneously smoke any of the following vegetable casserole dishes with the main course of your meal, simply place the dish on the grill, under or next to the meat, and cook for the same length of time. Use chips or wood for any smoke flavor, and watch even guests who generally don't like vegetables devour the results.

Mixed Vegetable Montage

2 packages frozen mixed vegetables
1 package frozen cauliflower
20–30 fresh or canned mushrooms
1 can Cheddar cheese soup, undiluted
Salt and pepper to taste
¼ cup grated Parmesan cheese

Combine vegetables in ovenproof casserole dish, and pour soup over them. Season to taste with salt and pepper and sprinkle with cheese.

Courtesy of Bosman Industries, Inc.

Frozen Vegetables

Tear off a piece of heavy-duty aluminum foil about 12 to 18 inches long. Open a 10-ounce package of frozen vegetables and break into chunks or pieces in the center of the foil. Or pour out frozen vegetables from plastic bag. Dot with butter, season with salt and pepper, and sprinkle with 2 to 3 tablespoons of water. Bring sides of foil to center and fold over and over; fold ends of package to seal. Put on grill and smoke-cook along with meat or fish.

Courtesy of The Brinkmann Corporation

Winter Squash

Halve and seed medium acorn or hubbard squash, or scoop seeds from serving-size chunks of hubbard, butternut, or buttercup squash. Brush with butter and put on grill, cut side down. Smoke-cook about 2 hours or until tender.

Courtesy of The Brinkmann Corporation

Zucchini Boats

Halve several 6-inch zucchini. Brush with melted butter and sprinkle with salt and pepper. Grill over smoking embers until done.

Courtesy of Charcoal Briquet Institute

SAUCES

Basic Basting Sauce

⅓ cup wine vinegar
⅓ cup fresh lemon juice
⅓ cup salad oil
½ teaspoon soy sauce
Salt and pepper to taste

Combine ingredients and mix well. Use during cooking to baste meats or poultry. Makes 1 cup.

Courtesy of Metals Engineering Corporation

Basting Sauce for Fresh Fish

¼ stick butter
½ cup white wine
1 teaspoon rosemary
1 teaspoon fresh lemon juice

Melt the butter, stir in the wine, and add seasonings. Brush on fresh fish and apply again as needed to keep fish from drying out during cooking.

Courtesy of Charcoal Briquet Institute

Basting Sauce for Fowl

1 pound butter
⅔ cup sherry or red wine
2 tablespoons Worcestershire sauce
2 tablespoons soy sauce
2 cloves garlic, crushed
½ cup chopped parsley
2 teaspoons salt
1 cup water

Combine ingredients in heavy saucepan and bring to a boil. Lower heat and simmer for 30 minutes. Paint sauce on meat surfaces halfway through cooking and at end of cooking time. The above recipe will make enough sauce to cook 16 chickens or 4 turkeys; it is equally good when used to smoke any kind of beef, ham, pork, or lamb.

Courtesy of Bosman Industries, Inc.

Barbecue Marinade and Basting Sauce

3 8-ounce cans tomato sauce
1 small bottle Worcestershire sauce
¼ teaspoon garlic powder
½ pound butter
½ cup brown sugar
1 teaspoon dry mustard
2 tablespoons vinegar
2 tablespoons lemon juice
⅛ teaspoon red pepper
½ teaspoon salt
½ teaspoon seasoned pepper

Simmer all ingredients for 30 minutes in heavy pan, stirring occasionally. Brush on ribs, chops, steaks, or chicken as it cooks, and baste several times.

Courtesy of Bosman Industries, Inc.

Barbecue Sauce

1 tablespoon chopped onion
1 tablespoon fat
½ clove garlic
1 can tomato paste
½ cup water
2 teaspoons sugar
¼ teaspoon salt
¼ teaspoon chili powder
¼ teaspoon paprika
1 teaspoon Worcestershire sauce
2 tablespoons vinegar
1 tablespoon prepared mustard
2 tablespoons catsup

Sauté onion in fat over low heat until it is soft but not brown. Peel garlic and add to onions. Add remaining ingredients. Mix thoroughly. Bring to boiling point, lower heat, and simmer for 10 minutes. Remove garlic and pour over meat or poultry.

Courtesy of Cooperative Extension Service, University of Alaska

Barbecue Sauce

3 8-ounce cans tomato sauce
1 small bottle Worcestershire sauce
¼ teaspoon garlic powder
½ pound butter
½ cup brown sugar
1 teaspoon dry mustard
2 tablespoons vinegar
2 tablespoons lemon juice
⅛ teaspoon red pepper
½ teaspoon salt
½ teaspoon seasoned pepper

Mix all ingredients and simmer for 30 minutes.

Courtesy of Bosman Industries, Inc.

Berried Ham Sauce

1 pound fresh cranberries
1 cup maple syrup

Cook mixture together until the cranberries split. Push through a sieve. Spread on cooked ham.

Courtesy of McArthur's Smokehouse

Burgundy Bing Ham Glaze

1 1-pound can bing cherries
2 tablespoons cornstarch
¾ cup burgundy
2 tablespoons wine vinegar
¼ cup light corn syrup
2 teaspoons lemon juice

Take ¾ cup juice from can of cherries and mix in with the cornstarch, stirring until the mixture is smooth. Add the burgundy, vinegar, and corn syrup, and bring to a boil, stirring all the while. Mix in lemon juice slowly. Glaze ham with ½ cup of mixture; at serving time, add cherries to rest of sauce and heat slowly.

Courtesy of McArthur's Smokehouse

Gold Rush Sauce

¼ cup prepared mustard
1 tablespoon sugar
1 tablespoon minced onion
2 tablespoons Worcestershire sauce
1 tablespoon catsup
1½ teaspoons salt
⅛ teaspoon garlic powder
⅛ teaspoon cayenne pepper
½ pound butter, softened

Combine all ingredients except butter. Add gradually to butter, mixing thoroughly. Grill steaks or hamburgers on one side, turn, and spread mixture on cooked side. Do same with other side when cooked. Also tastes great on chicken.

Courtesy of R. T. French Company

Gourmet Steak Sauce

¼ cup finely chopped green onions
1 tablespoon butter
⅓ cup teriyaki sauce
¼ cup catsup
1 tablespoon dry mustard
1 teaspoon black pepper

Sauté green onions in butter; stir in remaining ingredients and heat. Serve warm over steaks or other cuts of beef.

Courtesy of Kikkoman International Inc.

Marmalade Magic Sauce

1 cup dark corn syrup
½ cup orange marmalade
2 teaspoons dry mustard

Mix well and use to glaze cooked ham.

Courtesy of McArthur's Smokehouse

McArthur's Hawaii Glaze for Ham

¾ cup strained honey
¾ cup pineapple juice
½ teaspoon dry mustard

Place ingredients in a saucepan and stir over low heat until thick enough to spread easily. Glaze cooked ham with sauce.

Courtesy of McArthur's Smokehouse

Mint-the-Meat Sauce

1 cup oil
½ cup wine vinegar
¼ cup Worcestershire sauce
1½ teaspoons crushed mint flakes
1 teaspoon crushed thyme
1 teaspoon black pepper
1 teaspoon paprika
½ teaspoon salt

Combine ingredients. Pour over lamb chops, a roast, or kebab cubes. Let stand for 2 hours before cooking. Drain meat, saving liquid for basting. Baste frequently while grilling or roasting.

Courtesy of R. T. French Company

Oil Garlic Sauce

½ pint cooking oil
1 tablespoon salt
1 teaspoon black pepper
1 tablespoon Worcestershire sauce
3 cloves garlic, minced

Place in closed container and shake vigorously to blend. Place meat on forked stick or spit and broil over hot coals for 20 to 25 minutes, brushing liberally with sauce. Use either a brush or cheesecloth fastened at the end of a stick for spreading the sauce.

Courtesy of Cooperative Extension Service, University of Alaska

Polynesian Teriyaki Sauce

½ cup teriyaki sauce
⅓ cup apricot-pineapple preserves
½ teaspoon ginger
⅛ teaspoon garlic powder
1 tablespoon cornstarch
¼ cup water

Combine first 4 ingredients in saucepan; bring to a boil slowly. Meanwhile, combine cornstarch and water; add to sauce. Cook until sauce thickens. Serve over grilled steaks, burgers, chicken, or fish.

Courtesy of Kikkoman International Inc.

Sauce for Smoked Ham

1 cup brown sugar
½ cup vinegar
½ cup water
⅓ cup dry mustard
2 teaspoons flour
1 teaspoon beef extract
2 egg yolks

Place all ingredients except egg yolks in top of double boiler. Mix and blend slowly. Then add and blend yolks, cooking slowly until thick. Serve chilled, or at room temperature.

Courtesy of Mrs. Robert Thrun/McArthur's Smokehouse

Shiny Citrus Sauce

Bring 1 cup water, ½ cup soy sauce, and ¼ cup lime marmalade to boil over medium heat until marmalade dissolves. Combine 3 tablespoons cornstarch with ¼ cup water; add to sauce mixture and cook until sauce thickens. Stir in 1½ teaspoons grated lemon rind. Serve over grilled bullheads, blue gills, perch, or other small whole fish.

Courtesy of Kikkoman International Inc.

Sizzle Sauce

Suited to either meat or fish, this sauce creates a rich brown glaze on the food as it cooks.

½ cup Worcestershire sauce
¼ cup lemon juice
¼ cup oil
¼ teaspoon garlic powder
⅛ teaspoon cayenne pepper

Combine ingredients. Use to baste meat while grilling or broiling.

Courtesy of R. T. French Company

Sugar-Foot Sauce

1 can (1 pound) jellied cranberry sauce or currant jelly
¼ cup Worcestershire sauce

Melt cranberry sauce over low heat, stirring with a fork to speed melting. Blend in Worcestershire sauce. Grill precooked ham slices until nearly done, then baste with sauce. Also good on chicken.

Courtesy of R. T. French Company

Top Tomato Sauce

¾ cup catsup
2 tablespoons sweet pepper flakes
2 tablespoons brown sugar
1 tablespoon minced onion
2 tablespoons butter
2 tablespoons prepared mustard
1 teaspoon salt

Combine ingredients in a saucepan. Bring to a boil, lower heat, and simmer for 10 minutes. Serve hot over frankfurters, hamburgers, broiled chicken, or spareribs.

Courtesy of R. T. French Company

COOKING
FOR A CROWD

As any experienced backyard chef knows, cooking for a sizeable group of people can often be a monumental task. Even though some large models of grills and cookers can hold numerous cuts of meat and side dishes at one time, a sudden party or a family reunion can tax even the most efficient backyard cooking apparatus.

Products that add smoke flavor to foods can readily solve this problem, giving the cook a chance to prepare group feasts indoors in a kitchen, without the pressure of watching the fire or the fuel (a special blessing on rainy days).

The following recipes call for Bar-B-Q Liquid Smoke, a product manufactured by the E. H. Wright Company, and made by condensing and distilling pure smoke from the burning of green hickory trees. The company also produces a similar product for use directly on foods at the table—Table Smoke.

Both ingredients are available in local gourmet shops and some supermarkets. You can, of course, experiment with this product in lesser degrees by simply cutting down the quantity of the ingredients in any of these recipes. To obtain a free recipe book on other suggestions for this special kind of Smoke Cookery, write to E. H. Wright Company, Kansas City, Missouri 64108.

Baked Beans

5 pounds navy beans
2½ pounds salt pork, cubed
2 cups brown sugar
½ cup molasses
3 tablespoons salt
2 tablespoons vinegar
1½ cups finely chopped onion
2 tablespoons Liquid Smoke
1½ gallons hot water

Soak beans overnight. Drain. Fry cubed salt pork until brown. Mix pork cubes and pork drippings with sugar, molasses, salt, vinegar, onion, and smoke seasoning. Add this mixture to the beans, mixing well. Pour into large roasting pan. Add water. Cover and bake for 7 to 8 hours at 250°F. Uncover and brown the last hour. Add extra water during baking as needed. If more flavor is desired, add strips of bacon on top for the last hour of baking. *(25–30 servings)*

Courtesy of E. H. Wright Company, Inc.

...ked Stuffed Peppers

...whole green peppers
...quarts finely ground cooked beef, veal, or
...m
...art raw rice
...arts boiling water
...blespoon salt
...p ground onion
...cups fat or oil for onion
3⅔ quarts whole kernel corn
1½ quarts beef stock
1 tablespoon Liquid Smoke
2½ cups bread crumbs
⅓ cup fat or oil for crumbs

Wash peppers. Cut off stem ends, removing seeds and membranes. Pour boiling water over them for about 10 minutes. Cook rice in salted boiling water. When tender, drain but do not rinse. Brown onions in fat. Mix ground meat, onions, rice, and corn with beef stock to which Liquid Smoke has been added and blend until well mixed and of right consistency. Fill peppers and place in pans for baking. Mix bread crumbs with fat and sprinkle over each pepper. Add water to cover bottom of pans. Bake at 350°F. for 35 to 45 minutes or until brown. *(50 servings)*

Courtesy of E. H. Wright Company, Inc.

Barbecued Brisket of Beef

20 pounds brisket of beef
½ cup vinegar
1 tablespoon barbecue spice
¼ cup salt
1 whole onion
¼ cup shrimp spice
1 cup Liquid Smoke
1 clove garlic, crushed
2 cups barbecue sauce

Wash brisket in cold water. Place in kettle, cover with cold water, and add all of the ingredients. Simmer until tender, about 2½ to 3 hours. Remove from kettle. Brush on or sprinkle with additional Liquid Smoke. Pour on barbecue sauce. Place in large baking pan. Bake 20 minutes at 375°F. *(40 servings)*

Courtesy of E. H. Wright Company, Inc.

Browned Rice

1¾ quarts raw rice
2½ cups butter
3 quarts finely chopped onion
3 tablespoons salt
1 tablespoon garlic salt
½ teaspoon pepper
6 quarts beef stock
1 tablespoon Liquid Smoke

Melt butter in frying pan. Add rice, onion, salt, garlic salt and pepper, and fry until golden brown. Heat beef stock to which Liquid Smoke has been added. Add rice to hot stock and simmer until rice is cooked and liquid is absorbed. *(40 servings)*

Courtesy of E. H. Wright Company, Inc.

Chili con Carne

4 pounds dry kidney beans (or 1½ #10 cans kidney beans)
1½ cups finely chopped onion
¼ cup shortening or drippings
9 pounds ground beef
3 tablespoons MSG
1 #10 can tomato juice
2¼ quarts tomato puree
4⅔ cups water or stock
¾ cup brown sugar
1½ teaspoons cayenne
½ cup chili powder
4½ tablespoons salt
2 tablespoons Liquid Smoke

Pick over beans and wash well. Soak overnight in cold water to cover. (Omit this process for canned beans.) Drain. Add cold water and cook until just tender. Drain.

Sauté onions in shortening. Mix ground beef with MSG. Add onions. Brown the meat mixture. Add beans, tomato juice, tomato puree, and water or stock. Simmer. Add brown sugar and seasonings. Simmer for one hour. *(48 servings)*

Courtesy of E. H. Wright Company, Inc.

Franks and Beans

100 frankfurters
4 #10 cans baked beans
2 cups molasses
2 tablespoons Liquid Smoke
1 cup brown sugar
1 cup finely chopped onion

Combine beans with all the other ingredients except the franks, mixing well. Place bean mixture in two large roasting pans, spreading evenly. Place franks on top of beans, pushing them down in the beans so they will be mostly under the surface. Bake at 350°F. for one hour or until browned and hot. *(50 servings)*

Courtesy of E. H. Wright Company, Inc.

Meat Loaf

8 pounds ground beef
2½ pounds ground pork
5 cups soft bread crumbs
10 eggs
2½ cups chopped onion
2½ cups chopped celery
2½ cups catsup
2 tablespoons salt
1¼ teaspoons pepper
1½ tablespoons Liquid Smoke

Thoroughly blend meat with crumbs, eggs, vegetables, catsup, and seasonings. Divide into 6 9x4½x2¾ loaf pans. Bake in 325°F. oven for 1½ hours. *(54 servings)*

Courtesy of E. H. Wright Company, Inc.

Mixed Vegetable Casserole

1¾ quarts chopped carrots
2½ quarts chopped celery
3 quarts beef stock
3 cups chopped onion
2 cups chopped green pepper
½ cup butter
1½ quarts cooked peas

Cook carrots and celery in beef stock until tender. Drain, reserving stock. Sauté onion and peppers in butter. Set aside with cooked peas.

Sauce

1 cup butter
3 cups flour
1 gallon liquid made up of reserved beef stock
   from cooking vegetables plus milk
2 tablespoons salt
1 teaspoon pepper
1 tablespoon Liquid Smoke
2 quarts grated Cheddar cheese
Buttered bread crumbs

Melt butter. Add flour and let cook a few minutes, stirring slowly. Do not brown. Add liquid, stirring rapidly until boiling. Cook for about 5 minutes. Add all seasonings. When thick, add cheese and cook until cheese melts. Add vegetables, mixing thoroughly. Place in greased baking pans. Sprinkle with buttered bread crumbs. Bake at 375°F. until brown. *(50 servings)*

Courtesy of E. H. Wright Company, Inc.

Navy Beans

10 pounds navy beans
3 gallons water
1 large onion
¼ pound salt pork
½ cup salt
1 teaspoon pepper
1 tablespoon Liquid Smoke

Soak beans overnight in water. Combine all ingredients; add more water if necessary. Simmer until done (2 to 3 hours). Serve with ham hocks or cubes of ham. *(50 servings)*

Courtesy of E. H. Wright Company, Inc.

Hot Potato Salad

10 pounds potatoes
1 pound onions, chopped
½ cup chopped parsley
1 quart diced celery
1½ pounds bacon, diced
1 cup vinegar
3¾ cups water
⅓ cup sugar
1½ tablespoons salt
½ teaspoon white pepper
1 teaspoon Liquid Smoke

Scrub potatoes and cook unpeeled until done. Peel and dice while hot. Mix in onions, parsley, and celery. Fry bacon until crispy but not hard. Add bacon plus fat from bacon to the vinegar, water, sugar, salt, pepper, and smoke seasoning. Pour this over the hot potato mixture and mix lightly but thoroughly. Let stand at least an hour to season throughout. Serve hot. For additional color, add a small can of pimientos. *(25 servings)*

Courtesy of E. H. Wright Company, Inc.

Salmon Patties

8 pounds canned salmon
2¾ quarts bread crumbs
1⅓ quarts finely cut cooked celery
1½ cups finely cut cooked onions
1 teaspoon paprika
3 tablespoons salt
11 eggs
2 cups milk (more or less) depending on amount
   of liquid in salmon)
2 teaspoons Liquid Smoke

Break salmon apart, separate, removing bones
and skin. Mix salmon, bread crumbs, cooked celery and onions, paprika, and salt. Beat eggs well,
add milk and Liquid Smoke. Mix with salmon
mixture. Shape into 4-ounce patties early in the
day, or the night before, and refrigerate. When
ready to serve, roll in flour, dip in beaten egg
and then in bread crumbs. Deep-fry until golden
brown. *(40 servings)*

Courtesy of E. H. Wright Company, Inc.

Smoked Country Sausage

85 pounds lean pork
15 pounds beef
1½ or 2 pounds salt
4 ounces black pepper
1 ounce red pepper
1 ounce mace
1 ounce sweet marjoram

Thoroughly mix seasoning ingredients. Cut meat in small pieces, spread out on a table, and sprinkle seasoning over it. Then run it through the grinder, using the small plate, and mix into it thoroughly 3 or 4 large tablespoons of smoke flavoring for each 50 pounds of meat. Stuff into casings. Lay sausages away in a cool place for 24 to 36 hours. Then put them in smoke flavoring for about 30 minutes, drain well and hang up to dry. A week later, dip them again, and hang for another week. (Ten minutes is long enough for the second dipping.) Then they are ready to cook. *(400 one-by-three-inch sausages)*

Courtesy of E. H. Wright Company, Inc.

Summer Sausage

15 pounds pork trimmings
25 pounds well-cured beef
6 ounces white pepper
½ pound salt
1 ounce black peppercorns
1 ounce whole mustard seed

Put meat through grinder; then add spices. Mix until evenly seasoned. Spread out in cool place and leave for 36 hours. Then stuff into hog casings and let hang for 12 or 24 hours. Smoke sausage three times, a week apart. Hang up until thoroughly dry and ready for use.

No harm is done if sausage becomes slightly

moldy. Simply wipe off casings and the product is as good as ever. *(160 one-by-three-inch sausages)*

Courtesy of E. H. Wright Company, Inc.

Smoky Cheese Spread

4 pounds Cheddar cheese
1 pound sour cream
1 cup mayonnaise
1 tablespoon Liquid Smoke
2 tablespoons Worcestershire sauce
2 tablespoons Tabasco sauce
2 tablespoons seasoning salt
1 small onion, minced

Shred cheese and let stand at room temperature until soft enough to work in remaining ingredients. Mix sour cream, mayonnaise, seasonings, and onion together. Add softened cheese and work until well mixed and fairly smooth. Serve with melba toast or assorted crackers. *(5 pounds)*

Courtesy of E. H. Wright Company, Inc.

Tuna Fish and Noodle Casserole

9½ pounds tuna fish, drained
3 pounds noodles
3 cups tuna oil, reserved from cans
3 cups flour
1½ tablespoons salt
2 tablespoons Liquid Smoke
1½ gallons milk, scalded
1 cup chopped green pepper
1 cup chopped onion
1 pound shredded Cheddar cheese

Cook noodles according to package directions. Drain. Make a sauce with tuna oil and flour. Let cook for 2 minutes. Add salt and smoke seasoning to milk. Add to roux and cook until thickened. Cook onions and peppers in salted water until tender. Drain. Add to sauce. Arrange noodles and tuna fish in well-greased baking pans. Cover with sauce evenly. Sprinkle shredded cheese over the top of each pan. Bake at 375°F. for 20 to 30 minutes or until browned. *(40–50 servings)*

Courtesy of E. H. Wright Company, Inc.

Appendix

Sources of Mail Order Smoked Foods

The Great Valley Mills
Quakertown
Bucks County,
Pennsylvania 18951

Smoked turkey, country
sausage, dried beef,
bologna

Harrington's
Richmond,
Vermont 05477

Smoked ham, Canadian
bacon, dried beef, pork
loins, sausage, turkey,
duck, pheasant

ITT Gwaltney Inc.
Smithfield,
Virginia 23430

Smoked ham, bacon,
sausage

McArthur's Smokehouse
Millerton,
New York 12546

Smoked hams, bacon,
sausage, pork loins, roasts,
turkey, Cornish game
hens, capon, beef, corned
beef, lamb, trout

Nodine's Smokehouse
Route 63
Goshen,
Connecticut 06756

Smoked ham, bacon, beef,
chicken, turkey, Cornish
game hens, capon, eels,
sausage, cheese

Smithfield Ham and
Products Co.
Smithfield,
Virginia 23430

Smoked ham products,
deviled ham spread, James
River and Amber Brand
products

Spruce Farm Smokehouse
Pine Plains,
New York 12567

Smoked sausage, eel, trout,
mackerel, bacon, ham,
cheese

The Swiss Colony
1112 7th Avenue
Monroe,
Wisconsin 53567

Smoked ham, sausage,
turkey, bacon

Vermont Casual House
143 Main Street
Brattleboro,
Vermont 05301

Smoked cheese, ham,
bacon, salami

The Wisconsin Cheeseman
P.O. Box 1
Madison,
Wisconsin 53701

Smoked sausage, bacon,
ham, pheasant, turkey,
Cornish game hens

Directory of Manufacturers and Sources of Smokers

L. L. Bean
Freeport,
Maine 04033

Electric smokers, camp
stoves, charcoal grills

Bosman Industries, Inc.
2114 Seymour
P.O. Box 4342
Shreveport,
Louisiana 71104

Cook 'N Ca'Jun Charcoal-
Water Smoker and
accessories

The Brinkmann
Corporation
4215 McEwen Road
Dallas,
Texas 75240

Smoke 'N Pit Charcoal
and Electric Water
Smokers and accessories

Charmglow Products P.O. Box 127 Bristol, Wisconsin 53104	Charmglow Gas Grills and accessories
Colonial Garden Kitchens 270 West Merrick Road Valley Stream, New York 11582	Outers Electric Smoker
Husky Industries 62 Perimeter Center East Atlanta, Georgia 30346	Charcoal Briquets, Hickory Chips, Hardwood Briquets
Luhr Jensen and Sons, Inc. Hood River, Oregon 97031	Little Chief Electric Smokers and accessories
Metals Engineering Corp. P.O. Box 3005 Greeneville, Tennessee 37743	Meco Charcoal Grills and accessories
Neosho Products Company P.O. Box 622 Neosho, Missouri 64850	Buddy L Grills and accessories
Oster Corporation 5055 North Lydell Avenue Milwaukee, Wisconsin 53217	Electric Meat Grinders and Sausage Making Kits
3M Company 3M Center Saint Paul, Minnesota 55101	Heavy-Duty Grill Scrubber
Turco Manufacturing Company 501 South Line Street DuQuoin, Illinois 62832	Charette and Malibu Gas and Electric Grills

W. C. Bradley Co.
1442 Belfast Avenue
Columbus,
Georgia 31904

Char-Broil Charcoal and
Gas Cookers

Index

About the Author

Georgia Orcutt teaches free-lance writing in the Boston area. The author of a book on planters and the editor of two travel guides to New England and New York State, Ms. Orcutt is currently the editor of the *Yankee Press*. She lives outside of Boston with her husband and her three Irish wolfhounds.